REDEMPTION AND RESTORATION

Reversing Life's Greatest Losses

A Study of Ruth and Esther

D0972499

Jack W. Hayford

with

Kathy A. Hagan

THOMAS NELSON PUBLISHERS

Nashville • Atlanta • London • Vancouver

Redemption and Restoration:
Reversing Life's Greatest Losses
Copyright © 1996 by Jack W. Hayford

Published in Nashville, Tennessee, by Thomas Nelson, Inc.

Unless otherwise indicated, Scripture quotations are from the
New King James Version of the Bible, © 1979, 1980, 1982,
Thomas Nelson, Inc., Publishers

Printed in the United States of America
2 3 4 5 6 7 8 — 01 00 99 98 97 96

CONTENTS

Redemption and Restoration: Reversing Life's Greatest Losses is one of a series of study guides that focus exciting, discovery-geared coverage of Bible book and power themes—all prompting toward dynamic, Holy Spirit-filled living.

About the Executive Editor

JACK W. HAYFORD, noted pastor, teacher, writer, and composer, is the Executive Editor of the complete series, working with the publisher in conceiving and developing each of the books.

Dr. Hayford is Senior Pastor of The Church On The Way, the First Foursquare Church of Van Nuys, California. He and his wife, Anna, have four married children, all of whom are active in either pastoral ministry or vital church life. As General Editor of the *Spirit-Filled Life Bible*, Pastor Hayford led a four-year project, which has resulted in the availability of one of today's most practical and popular study Bibles. He is author of more than twenty books, including *A Passion for Fullness, The Beauty of Spiritual Language, Rebuilding the Real You,* and *Prayer Is Invading the Impossible.* His musical compositions number over four hundred songs, including the widely sung "Majesty."

About the Writer

KATHY A. HAGAN is currently Associate Pastor at Cobblestone Church of God in Madison, Mississippi. In addition to a variety of pastoral duties, she administrates the programs of discipleship and Christian education and teaches community Bible studies.

Kathy holds both undergraduate and graduate degrees in education from Murray State University and was a public school teacher in Tennessee for sixteen years. She received the Master of Divinity degree in 1994 from the Church of God School of Theology in Cleveland, Tennessee. As a graduating senior at that institution, Kathy was recipient of the Pentecostal Ministry Award which is given for academic scholarship, Christian character, contribution to the seminary community, and promise for future Pentecostal ministry.

Kathy has a grown son and daughter-in-law, Jeff and Lori Hagan, who reside in Charleston, South Carolina.

THE GIFT
THAT KEEPS ON GIVING

One of the most precious gifts God has given us is His Word, the Bible. Wrapped in the glory and sacrifice of His Son and delivered by the power and ministry of His Spirit, it is a treasured gift—the gift that keeps on giving, because the Giver it reveals is inexhaustible in His love and grace.

Tragically, though, fewer and fewer people are opening this gift and seeking to understand what it's all about and how to use it. They often feel intimidated by it. It requires some assembly, and its instructions are hard to comprehend sometimes. How does the Bible fit together anyway? What does this ancient Book have to say to us who are looking toward the twenty-first century?

Will taking the time and energy to understand its instructions and to fit it all together really help you and me?

Yes. Yes. Without a shred of doubt.

The *Spirit-Filled Life Bible Discovery Guide* series is designed to help you unwrap, assemble, and enjoy all God has for you in the pages of Scripture. It will focus your time and energy on the books of the Bible, the people and places they describe, and the themes and life applications that flow thick from its pages like honey oozing from a beehive.

So you can get the most out of God's Word, this series has a number of helpful features:

 WORD WEALTH

"WORD WEALTH" provides definitions of key terms.

BEHIND THE SCENES

"BEHIND THE SCENES" supplies information about cultural practices, doctrinal disputes, business trades, etc.

AT A GLANCE

"AT A GLANCE" features helpful maps and charts.

BIBLE EXTRA

"BIBLE EXTRA" will guide you to other resources that will enable you to glean more from the Bible's wealth.

PROBING THE DEPTHS

"PROBING THE DEPTHS" will explain controversial issues raised by particular lessons and cite Bible passages and other sources to help you come to your own conclusions.

FAITH ALIVE

The "FAITH ALIVE" feature will help you see and apply the Bible to your day-to-day needs.

The only resources you need to complete and apply these study guides are a heart and mind open to the Holy Spirit, a prayerful attitude, and a pencil and a Bible. Of course, you may draw upon other sources, but these study guides are comprehensive enough to give you all you need to gain a good, basic understanding of the Bible book being covered and how you can apply its themes and counsel to your life.

A word of warning, though. By itself, Bible study will not transform your life. It will not give you power, peace, joy, comfort, hope, and a number of other gifts God longs for you to unwrap and enjoy. Through Bible study, you will grow in your understanding of the Lord, His kingdom and your place in it, but you must be sure to rely on the Holy Spirit to guide your study and your application of the Bible's truths. He, Jesus promised, was sent to teach us "all things" (John 14:26; cf. 1 Cor. 2:13). Bathe your study time in prayer, asking the Spirit of God to illuminate the text, enlighten your mind, humble your will, and comfort your heart. He will never let you down.

My prayer and goal for you is that as you unwrap and begin to explore God's Book for living His way, the Holy Spirit will fill every fiber of your being with the joy and power God longs to give all His children. So read on. Be diligent. Stay open and submissive to Him. You will not be disappointed. He promises you!

Lesson 1/Sojourn in Moab: Colliding with Chaos (Ruth 1:1–5)

CHAOS . . . Utter disorder and terrifying confusion.
A world spun out of control.
Life on the edge, hanging by a thread.
Everything turned upside down.

CHAOS . . . Order displaced by a swirling , dizzying mass of events screaming for a word of continuity.
A mutiny against meaning.
Life that doesn't play by the rules.

CHAOS . . . Open-mouthed, silent screaming, when heaven seems deaf and God is unsearchable.
Despair unleashed.
The dark terror before dawn's light.

CHAOS . . . Life's events gone haywire.

CHAOS . . . Elimelech's plan turned sour.

CHAOS . . . Naomi, empty-handed, stranded in a foreign land.

The five opening verses of chapter 1 seem to cry out to have added to their conclusion a *selah*—"Pause and think of this!" Within their words lies a picture of chaos. Yet, the writer's terse, objective reporting of Naomi's years of devastation and multiple losses may too quickly and too easily be passed over by the reader. These horrendous events may be heard with the same emotional detachment with which Americans are prone to view the six o'clock news. Like Job's compounded tragedies, Naomi's losses are stacked one upon another. They beg to be unraveled and assessed so that shape and understanding may be given to the horror of the chaotic events surrounding the sojourn in Moab.

AN ERA OF CHAOS AND CONFUSION (1:1a)

The Book of Ruth is situated in the second division of the Old Testament among the twelve books which record the history of the nation of Israel. The opening verse succinctly identifies the time in which the story of Ruth unfolds by simply stating: "Now it came to pass in the days when the judges ruled." This statement places the events recorded in Ruth in the same time frame as the Book of Judges, between 1380 and 1050 B.C. The Book of Ruth was not written down, however, until about 990 B.C., some time after David became king. Although some scholars suggest that the prophet Samuel may have written Ruth, its author is unknown.[1]

 AT A GLANCE

THE MAJOR DIVISIONS OF THE OLD TESTAMENT	
I. Books of the Pentateuch, or the Law	Genesis through Deuteronomy
II. Books about the History of Israel	**Joshua through Esther**
III. Books of Wisdom Writings	Job through Song of Solomon
IV. Books of the Major Prophets	Isaiah through Daniel
V. Books of the Minor Prophets	Hosea through Malachi

BOOKS ABOUT THE HISTORY OF ISRAEL[2]	
Book	Summary
Joshua	The capture and settlement of the Promised Land
Judges	The nation of Israel is rescued by a series of judges, or military leaders
Ruth	**A beautiful story of God's love and care**
1 and 2 Samuel	The early history of Israel, including the reigns of Saul and David

1 and 2 Kings	A political history of Israel, focusing on the reigns of selected kings from the time of Solomon to the captivity of the Jewish people by Babylon
1 and 2 Chronicles	A religious history of Israel, covering the same period of time as 2 Samuel and 1 and 2 Kings
Ezra	The return of the Jewish people from captivity in Babylon
Nehemiah	The rebuilding of the walls of Jerusalem after the exiles returned from Babylon
Esther	God's care for His people under Gentile rule

The period when the judges ruled was a turbulent and chaotic time. Life in Israel was characterized by repeated cycles of idolatry, sin, and oppression followed by repentance, deliverance, and temporary peace.

 BIBLE EXTRA

Read the following verses and record the events which mark the beginning and the ending of the era of the judges.
Judges 1:1

1 Samuel 3:19, 20

Look up the following references and jot down what each reveals about the days when the judges ruled.
The first generation (Judg. 2:10)

A habitual activity (Judg. 2:11; 3:7, 12; 4:1)

A continuing fact (Judg. 17:6; 18:1; 19:1)

A concluding summary (Judg. 21:25)

FAITH ALIVE

Given the above facts, list at least three ways in which our contemporary era is like the days of the judges.

1.

2.

3.

In such an era, it is easy to be distracted and pulled away by a proliferation of ungodly influences. The ethics and pattern of the Christian lifestyle are not the norm. Compromises are easy to make since such steps away from God-centered life cause one to "fit" more comfortably in society's mainstream.

How has living in such an era affected you personally? In what way(s) are you compromising in the area of lifestyle? Ethics? Family relationships? Personal devotion to God? Witness?

THE BEGINNING OF NAOMI'S SORROWS (1:1,2)

Verses 1 and 2 record the events which mark the beginning of Naomi's day of sorrow. Like the unstable nation of Israel, the family of Elimelech is plunged into a "riches-to-rags" story.

Where did the tragic events which form the background of this story begin, and where did they unfold? (vv. 1b, 2)

At a Glance

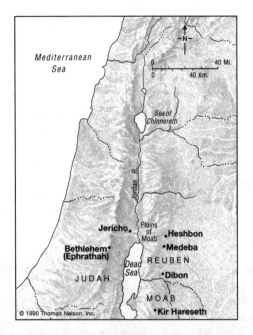

From Bethlehem, Judah, to the land of Moab. The land allotted to the tribe of Judah in the Promised Land is described in Joshua 15:1–12. Bounded by the Mediterranean Sea on the east and the Dead Sea on the west, Judah was the southernmost tribe of Israel with the exception of Simeon. Although not far from Judah, apparently Moab had not been affected by the famine—whatever its cause may have been. Moab's terrain was mainly high plateau land. It was a fertile region yielding both croplands and pastures.[3]

Word Wealth

Elimelech's intentions in leaving Judah to live in Moab are clearly seen in the verb used in verse 1. There, **dwell,** *gur*, means to lodge somewhere, to temporarily reside; to dwell as a stranger among other people; to be a guest or an alien in a particular land; to have a temporary resident's status (see Jer.

42:17).[4] Possibly Elimelech planned to sojourn as a migrant worker until the famine ended in Bethlehem.

AT A GLANCE

Study the chart below. List any additional losses you think Naomi and her family may have experienced as a result of the events recorded in Ruth 1:1, 2.

THE BEGINNING OF NAOMI'S SORROWS (1:1, 2)			
Verse	Event	Some Resulting Losses	Other Losses?
1	Famine in Bethlehem	Source of Income Means of Livelihood	
1, 2	Leaving Homeland	Friends and Extended Family Social/Religious Community and its Traditions Family Inheritance (Land)	

BEHIND THE SCENES

Famine was a continuing threat to the people living in Israel. Freedom from war and consistent, timely rainfall were imperative for crops to flourish in the semi-arid lands of Palestine (see Judg. 6:3–6). In the Mosaic Covenant, God provided protection for Israel from both of these causes of famine. He promised to bless Israel with intermittent and seasonal rains as a token of covenant harmony when she wholeheartedly loved and served Him (Deut. 11:13–15). God also pledged to protect Israel against her enemies and cause her to fully possess the land so that no one was "able to stand against" Israel when she observed His commands and faithfully taught them to the children (Deut. 11:22–25).

Was the famine which caused Elimelech to leave Judah a result of corporate sin? There is no way to know for sure.

But given Israel's history of recurring idolatry and disobedience during the days of the judges, it seems likely.

The Continuing Saga of Loss

It is not known how long Elimelech and his family lived in Moab before their former misfortunes were compounded by new tragedies. Grief was soon added to grief, and loss was added to loss.

 At a Glance

Study the chart. Fill in the missing parts. List any additional losses you think Naomi may have experienced as a result of the events recorded in Ruth 1:3–5.

NAOMI'S YEARS OF SORROW IN MOAB (Ruth 1:3–5)			
Event	Verse	Some Resulting Losses	Other Losses?
	3	Widowhood, Single Parenthood, Loss of Status	
	5	Loss of all Immediate Kin Life as an Unattached Female in a Patriarchal Society Loss of Protection for Old Age Loss of Continuing Lineage	

 Word Wealth

The vocabulary used in verse 4 indicates that Naomi may have suffered in another way during the interim between Elimelech's death and the deaths of Mahlon and Chilion. Although Elimelech had come to Moab as a temporary solution to the famine, it seems his sons had decided to make their home in Moab. The word **dwelt**, *yashab*, (v. 4) which describes the way the sons lived in Moab, means to sit down, stay, remain, continue, to marry, settle down permanently; to make one's home in a permanent location; to live.[5]

After Elimelech's death, Mahlon and Chilion joined themselves in a more permanent sense to the land of Moab. This action must have salted Naomi's grief with despair and disappointment. It meant Naomi might never return home to live in Judah. Nothing is stated directly in the text which indicates the extent to which Mahlon and Chilion accepted the culture and traditions of Moab. Perhaps the most that may be said is that, given their circumstances, Mahlon and Chilion gave up the hope of reclaiming their inheritance in Judah within their lifetime.

What two facts help to verify Mahlon and Chilion's permanent attachment to the land of Moab? (v. 4)

At the conclusion of verse 5, Naomi is truly empty-handed and stranded in a foreign land. Bereaved of husband and children, divested of material resources and status, deprived of the comfort of her homeland and kin, and too old to start over again, Naomi stands stripped to the bone by chaos. Her situation makes the reader want to shout: "Why has this happened to Naomi?"

 PROBING THE DEPTHS

The "Why" of Suffering: Christians in a severe or extended crisis like Naomi's are confronted by two questions: (1) How can a God who is both all-powerful and loving allow evil? and (2) Why do godly and sincere Christians experience what seems "cruel and unusual" suffering?

Job's story and that of the "Heroes of Enduring Faith" (Heb. 11:36-39) show that God does not always furnish the "why" of suffering. Scripture does, however, give some general answers to the often confounding dilemma. Study the references listed under the following headings.

1.   **The Curse**
     Genesis 3:14, 17–19
     John 14:30
2.   **We Await the Fulfillment of All Things**
     Romans 8:20–22
     1 Corinthians 15:21–24
     John 16:33
3.   **Unconfessed Personal or Corporate Sin**
     Judges 2:13–15
     Psalm 32:3–5
4.   **Foolishness**
     Psalm 38:2–5
     Proverbs 10:8, 13, 14
5.   **Direct Assault of Satan**
     John 10:10
     1 Peter 5:8

Was Naomi's situation just a chain of events beyond control or simply suffering common to humankind? Was the famine which initiated these events caused by corporate sin (Deut. 28:15, 16, 23, 24, 38–40)? Was this devastation a direct, vicious attack of Satan? Is Elimelech to blame for stubbornly making his own decisions without listening to God?

In retrospect, Elimelech's choice sure looks like a poor one! It is tempting to speculate that he lived in rebellion to his name ("My God is King") and therefore produced only that which was "weak or sickly" (Mahlon's name) and "failing or pining" (Chilion's name).[6] This principle could be validated by other Scripture. Corporate sin followed by human failure seems a logical conclusion. However, the text does not offer a solid answer. Perhaps the full complex of "whys" cannot be unraveled in this lifetime.

FAITH ALIVE

Most people can immediately find themselves somewhere in Naomi's story. All have experienced sorrow and pain. Some have known traumatic times of bereavement and loss which parallel Naomi's. Some are even now submerged in such crises. What should one do during such times? How can one respond to such devastation?

FINDING GOD'S HEALING FROM GRIEF AND LOSS

Step 1: Ask God to give you insight
Are the events caused by: [1] personal sin, [2] an ongoing pattern of unwise behavior, [3] satanic warfare, [4] the lack of wisdom or godliness of one in authority over you, [5] calamity caused by life in a sin-cursed world?

Step 2: Act on that insight
[1] *Sin:* Appropriate God's sanctifying power by confessing known sin, asking for cleansing, walking in the light of God's Word with sensitivity to the Holy Spirit (1 John 1:6, 7, 9). [2] *Behavior:* Fully define the pattern of behavior; uncover the "traps"— situations, persons, places which usually precede the behavior. Search the Scripture for the healthy alternative pattern of behavior. Submit yourself to God; practice the new behavior (Rom. 12:1, 2; Heb. 12:1; James 4:7, 8). [3] *Warfare:* Put on the armor of God, learn to wield the weapons of warfare. Ask for the anointing of the Spirit, be fervent in prayer in the understanding and in the Spirit. Ask others to stand with you (Eph. 6:10-18; Luke 11:3, 13; Rom. 8:26, 27). [4] *Another:* Submit yourself to God, pray for wisdom and healing. Lovingly confront the one in authority with the Word of God. Seek God for proper balance in following those in authority (1Pet. 5:5; 2 Tim. 3:16, 17; 4:2; 1 Cor. 5:11). [5] *Calamity:* Know that even the righteous are touched by it and that God experiences our pain. Ask for deliverance and comfort from God. Hold onto your faith. Allow others to comfort you (Job 2:11-13; Ps. 22:1-5, 12-18; Heb. 4:14-16).

Step 3: Understand that resolution of grief and loss is a process
Human beings generally go through several distinctive stages before reaching true grief and resolution: [1] *shock and denial,* usually a short-lived part of the process in which one refuses to believe what has happened. It may include bargaining with God; [2] *anger turned outward,* a reaction to the truth of the situation which is directed toward someone other than self and almost always includes some anger toward God; [3] *anger turned inward,* sadness and depression caused by a combination of false and true guilt which is usually worked through quickly; [4] *genuine grief,* a stage

which is vital to recovery and includes full expression of pain and loss; [5] *resolution*, healthy response which generally follows quickly after genuine grief is expressed. Here, joy and zest for living begin to return.[7]

Step 4: Choose to respond in a healthy way

People sometimes get "stuck" in a stage of the grieving process. One may become "paralyzed" by the events, bury emotions, or deny the full impact of the losses and remain in the first stage of denial. Some do not give up their anger toward someone or God and become bitter and unhappy. Others live in sadness or depression because they do not forgive or release themselves. They may live with a nebulous sense of condemnation, guilt, and the feeling of being separated from God's love.

How might a "false faith claim" that everything is okay hinder the healing process? In what stage of healing might this person become "stuck"?

How might the healing process be delayed if one takes an extreme view of 3 John 2 that the condition of the "soul" governs all outward and inward events and circumstances? In what stage might this person become "stuck"?

Have you, like Naomi, experienced multiple griefs and losses which left you feeling empty-handed, hollow, and helpless? When? Explain.

How would you describe your response to these losses? Did you tend to get bogged down at a certain point in the healing process?

How have you experienced a recovery from those losses?

BIBLE EXTRA

Like Naomi, Job experienced a series of unexplainable losses. Read Job 1:13–19; 2:7–9. Then read Job 42:10–17. Briefly describe below the reversal of loss which God worked in Job's life.

The key verse which underlines the message of the Book of Ruth is 2:12. Write that verse in your own words in the space below.

Now, scan Ruth 4:9, 10, 13–17. What do the key verse (2:12) and this passage in Ruth demonstrate about God's concern toward those who experience grief and loss? Record your thoughts in the space below.

Read Revelation 21:3–5. Describe below what this hope means to you.

FAITH ALIVE

Fortunately Naomi's story told in Ruth 1:1–5—like the story of Job or that of any servant of God—does not end with an account of losses. Its characters are woven into a drama of redemption and restoration. Its tragedies are transformed into triumphs. The displaced find a place in history. The empty one is made full; the barren is made fruitful. And the alien becomes the ancestor of a king of men and the King of kings!

Take time to thank God for being the God who brings order to chaos and reverses life's great losses. Thank Him for His faithful work in your life. You may wish to record your prayer below.

1. *Spirit-Filled Life Bible* (Nashville: Thomas Nelson Publishers, 1991), 343, "Judges: Introduction, Background." "Ruth, Book of," *Nelson's Illustrated Bible Dictionary* (Nashville: Thomas Nelson Publishers, 1986).

2. "Bible, The," *Nelson's Illustrated Bible Dictionary*.

3. *Spirit-Filled Life Bible*, 388, map. "Judah, Tribe of," *Nelson's Illustrated Bible Dictionary*. "Moab," *Nelson's Illustrated Bible Dictionary*.

4. *Spirit-Filled Life Bible*, 1119–1120, "Word Wealth: Jer. 42:17, dwell."

5. Ibid., 1152–1153, "Word Wealth: Lam: 5:19, remain."

6. Ibid., 388, note on Ruth 1:2. Ibid., 385–386, "Ruth: Introduction, Purpose."

7. Paul D. Meier, Frank B. Minirth, and Frank Wichern, *Introduction to Psychology and Counseling: Christian Perspectives and Applications* (Grand Rapids: Baker Book House, 1982), 266–276.

Lesson 2/Return to Judah: Facing Crisis with Faith and Commitment
(Ruth 1:5–22)

A cartoon pictures a young woman confiding to a marriage counselor: "I was looking for an ideal, I married an ordeal, and now I want a new deal!"[1] This play on words would be hilarious if it weren't for the fact that the philosophy it reflects concerning commitment in relationships is all too typical of modern society—churched and unchurched, Christian and non-Christian. Marriage, once perceived as a lifelong relationship, is often viewed today as a tentative attachment which can be easily dissolved for any number of reasons. And the rate of divorce among Christians closely parallels that of non-Christians. But the failure to make and maintain enduring commitments doesn't end there.

This lack of commitment is seen throughout every dimension of society. Parents "walk out" on their children at an alarming rate; children attach a note to an aging parent's sleeve and leave him or her sitting in a shopping mall. Sexual and physical abuse is at an all-time high. And abortion and euthanasia are considered viable options to dependent care.

With such failure to commit to immediate familial relationships, it is no wonder that deep attachments among the people of God often fail to form and some saints switch local congregations as easily as they change the flavor of their favorite ice cream. When the church they thought was "ideal" turns out to be made up of some members who can be real "ordeals," they too look for a "new deal."

In the first chapter of Ruth, the reader is confronted with an amazing picture of faith and personal commitment to relationship. There, Ruth fully embraces her mother-in-law in an indissoluble covenant. She does not tally the cost of continuing attachment to Naomi and her multiple losses or make her decision to follow Naomi to Judah in terms of personal advantage, convenience, or enjoyment. Thus, Ruth's beautiful story becomes an example to all who live in this age of dispensable commitments and throw away relationships.

CONFIDENT CONCLUSION (1:6, 7)

Verse 6 opens by stating of Naomi: "Then she arose." The decisiveness of her action is reminiscent of that of the four lepers of 2 Kings 7:3. As they sat starving outside the gate of Samaria, they said to one another: "Why are we sitting here until we die?" Like the lepers, Naomi did not know just how her help and deliverance would come. But she heard that God was once more moving in Bethlehem of Judah. So Naomi rose up from her despair. With faith's confidence, she moved toward God and home.

Write the phrase which tells why Naomi left Moab. (v.6)

BIBLE EXTRA

"The Lord had visited His people by giving them bread" (Ruth 1:6). This statement declares the answer to Bethlehem's famine and presents a solution for Naomi's plight. Throughout Old Testament history, the Lord visited His people when they cried out to Him. Here, the giving of bread speaks of the renewed fertility of the land and a supply of food (Ps. 132:15). Look up the following references to discover other results of a visitation of the Lord:

Exodus 3:16; 4:31

1 Samuel 2:21

Jeremiah 29:10; Zephaniah 2:7

Luke 1:68

In the New Testament, God's daily provision is "bread." Look up the following references and list things that may be considered bread.

Matthew 6:8, 11

Matthew 15:24–26

Luke 11:3, 13

Luke 22:19; Isaiah 53:4–6

John 6:33, 35, 38

COMPASSIONATE CONCERN (1:8–14)

To one passing by, it must have been a heartwrenching scene. On the dusty path which led toward Judah stood three women: one elderly, two young, all three widows. On their backs were the few things which they owned. Tears flowed down their cheeks. Their shoulders shook in rhythm with their sobs as they stood embracing one another.

Who were the women? (vv. 4, 8)

BEHIND THE SCENES

Names had more significance to people who lived during the eras depicted in the Old and New Testaments than they do to us today. The Hebrew *shem*, translated "name," suggests a "marking" or "branding." Thus, a name signified either one's present character, reputation, fame, authority, and accomplishments or what might be expected in one's future.[2] When character or status dramatically changed, a new name often accompanied the transformation. Abram became Abraham, Sarai became Sarah, and Jacob was changed to Israel (Gen. 17:5, 15; 32:26–28).

Examine the meanings of the names of the three women featured in this portion of Ruth:

Name	Meaning
Naomi	Pleasant, Delightful, Lovely
Orphah	Fawn
Ruth	Friendship, Female Friend[3]

 FAITH ALIVE

Based on what you just learned about names, answer the following questions:

If you chose a name for yourself which accurately "marked" your character and/or accomplishments today, what would it be?

What name might people at your workplace give you? What name would your spouse, children, or best friend choose to describe you?

Could you accurately be described as Friend? Pleasant/ Delightful? Fawn?

How would you like your "name" to change in the future? Take time to ask God to help you make that change.

Verses 8 and 9 record Naomi's first plea to her daughters-in-law as they stopped along the road a short while after beginning their trek to Bethlehem.

What command does Naomi give them? (v. 8)

What compliment does she offer her daughter-in-law? (v. 8)

What seems to be Naomi's main concern for Orpah and Ruth? (vv. 8, 9)

How did they respond to Naomi's entreaty? (v. 10)

 WORD WEALTH

In verses 8 and 9 Naomi fully releases Orpah and Ruth from any obligation to her. Not only does she command them to return to their mother's house, but she invokes a blessing upon them in doing so. A mother-in-law's deep affection and appreciation for her daughters-in-law is evidenced by the benediction Naomi offers in the name of the God of Israel. She asks that Orpah and Ruth experience her God's kindness and blessing. **Kindly,** *hesed,* (1:8) indicates a loyal, constant, protective love which would include the experience of God's goodness and His acts of deliverance and rescue.[4] **Rest,** *manoah,* (1:9) bears the

idea of a permanent resting place, security, and blessing especially as would be found in the protection of one's own home.
(See Ruth 3:1, which uses the same Hebrew word.)[5]

Naomi again attempts to persuade her daughters-in-law
with a second, more impassioned demand for their return to
Moab (vv. 11–13).

What reason for the young women's return does Naomi
emphasize in this plea?

BEHIND THE SCENES

Naomi's second plea for the young widows to return to
Moab may well reflect the fact that it would be much more difficult for a Moabite widow to "find rest" with a husband in
Judah. Although, technically, marriage between an Israelite
and a Moabite was permitted (Deut. 7:1–3), ethnic feelings
may have been a strong negative factor against such likeli-
hood. Throughout most of Israel's history, the Moabites were
Israel's enemies (Num. 22—25). During the times of the
judges, there was much turmoil between the nation of Israel
and Moab. Israel was relatively weak during this period.
Eglon, a king of Moab, began to oppress Israel, capturing ter-
ritory east of the Jordan River as far as Jericho. At one point,
Ehud the judge delivered Israel from Eglon (Judg. 3:12–30).
However, difficulty between the two nations continued through
the days of Israel's first kings.[6]

What were the results of Naomi's second speech? (v. 14)

How did Orphah's action confirm the accuracy of her
name?

CONFIRMED COMMITMENT (1:15–18)

Naomi tries one more time to persuade Ruth to join her sister-in-law before she is out of sight (v. 15). Naomi appeals to Ruth on the basis of her heritage, culture, and traditions.

If Ruth follows Orphah's example, to what and whom would she be returning? (v. 15)

Ruth responds with a powerful, often-quoted speech which silences any further protests Naomi could make. List four "I will" statements which underline Ruth's personal pledge to completely identify herself with Naomi. (vv. 16,17)

1.

2.

3.

4.

 WORD WEALTH

Ruth firmly declares: "Your people shall be my people, and your God, my God" (v. 16). **People,** *'am,* (1:15, 16) may be defined as a body of human beings unified as a nation. In contrast to *goi,* which may also be translated "people," *'am* indicates a people viewed from within the group.[7] Thus, Orphah was returning to her former life as one among her people and as one with them in their way of life. In vowing "Your people shall be my people," Ruth chose to live among the Judeans in Bethlehem even as Naomi will live. Ruth cuts herself off from her Moabite heritage and culture, clearly making herself an outsider to her former people. She chooses a new heritage in Judah and a new way of life—whatever it may bring.

In view of Ruth's refusal to obey Naomi's final plea to her (v. 15) and the "my people" and "my God" statements of verse 16, do you think Ruth's decision was based solely on friendship?

How does Ruth guarantee her pledge? (v. 17)

Like Orphah, Ruth lives up to her name. Read Proverbs 17:17 and describe how Ruth's action (vv. 14, 15) and her speech (vv. 16, 17) reflect the character portrayed in her name.

PROBING THE DEPTHS

Everyone has been asked the riddle: "Which came first, the chicken or the egg?" One might ask the same kind of question concerning Ruth's faith and commitment. Is Ruth's commitment first to Naomi and thus to her God? Is Ruth making a faith statement the foundation of her commitment to Naomi? Can Ruth's commitment to Naomi be separated from her commitment to Naomi's God?

Likewise, can faith in Jesus be separated from loving commitment to one's family? Can faith be separated from membership in the community of believers and commitment to them? Read 1 Timothy 5:8 and 1 John 4:7–16. Think about it!

FAITH ALIVE

With whom are you identified in an unshakable commitment? Your spouse? Parents? Children? Friend? Local church? Anyone?

What would it take to part you from that person(s)?

Who has pledged this kind of commitment to you?

Who has faithfully stood by you during times of grief and loss? When you were in the valley instead of on the mountaintop? Take time to thank God for the persons who are committed to you in relationship. Write a note to one of these people voicing your appreciation for their friendship and commitment.

What is your relationship to your in-laws? If the person who connects you to your in-laws died, how would your relationship with your in-laws change?

What is the basis of your commitments to others?

What is the level of your commitment to God? Would you describe yourself as an "acquaintance," a "fair weather friend," or a "tried and true" friend to God? On what basis can you make this evaluation?

CONFOUNDING SORROW (1:19–21)

The rest of Naomi and Ruth's journey to Bethlehem may have taken place in relative silence—a silence broken only by the necessity to communicate a few instructions directly related to the task at hand. Surely Naomi's mind must have been occupied with a recounting of the sad events of the past decade and the memory of her former manner of life in Bethlehem of

Judah. As the women of the city approach Naomi, her story spills out. Confounded and confused by the sorrows which have gripped her life, she utters a lament and accusation.

BEHIND THE SCENES

Verse 19 describes Naomi and Ruth's reception by the citizens of Bethlehem with words much like those of Matthew 21:10. What event is described in the Matthew passage?

The fact that "all the city was excited because of them" indicates that Naomi was indeed well known in the area. This manner of reception also suggests that Naomi's family occupied an important place in the community. Perhaps she was from a respected, leading family.[8] If this is true, the contrast between her present condition and her past position of dignity and honor would be even more painful.

The women's question recorded in verse 19 may indicate more than their joy at seeing Naomi. What else may be implied by their query?

AT A GLANCE

In verses 20 and 21, Naomi defines the transformation which has taken place in her with two statements of contrast. These statements indicate a change of character and condition.

NAOMI'S TRANSFORMATION		
Name	Naomi --------------------------➤	Mara
Character	Pleasant or Delightful -------➤	Bitter[9]
Condition	Full ----------------------------➤	Empty

List the four accusations Naomi raises against God concerning her sorrows. (vv. 20, 21). Add the complaint she uttered earlier (v. 13).

1. (v. 20)

2. (v. 21)

3. (v. 21)

4. (v. 21)

5. (v. 13)

 ## WORD WEALTH

The language Naomi uses for God offers an inside look at how she views God's activity in the recent string of tragic events. Up to this point Naomi has used "Yahweh" to name God. Now she introduces a new name. **Almighty,** *Shadday,* (v. 20), *Shaddai* (v. 21), describes God as all-mighty, unconquerable, the all-sufficient, all-powerful God who is eternally capable of being all that His people need.[10] Thus, she describes God in His omnipotence as One who could prevent her crises but who instead, she feels, has turned against her and afflicted her. She sees her sorrows as the direct activity of God.

In light of John 10:10, in what way is Naomi's understanding of God distorted by her calamity? (See also: "The 'Why' of Suffering," Lesson 1.)

What does Naomi's freedom to tell her story of tragedy suggest about her relationship with the women of Bethlehem? (vv. 20, 21)

How is the "heart" of these friends revealed in Ruth 4:14, 15, 17? How might their concern compare to God's concern for Naomi?

PROBING THE DEPTHS

Naomi's complaint against God. The question bound up in Naomi's complaints against God does not prove that she has turned from Him. She honestly admits her bitterness and despair. In her return, Naomi has moved in hope and faith even though she is confused and confounded by her situation, and also clearly confused about God's true nature. Though uttering complaints, Naomi moves in the right direction.

The very act of protest, when directed toward God, may be a sign of hope in His deliverance. The Psalms—noted for their expression of intimate relationship with God—contain many outcries against God and the circumstances of life. Psalms 22 and 88 specifically describe petitioners' sense of abandonment by God. Others voice descriptive complaints and feelings of despair (Ps. 74). Certainly God is not shocked by our thoughts and emotions (Ps. 139:1–4)!

Yet even the strongest laments recorded in Psalms are not totally engulfed in despair. It seems the very act of honest prayer is met by the Spirit's help, and hope is increased. Thus, questions and pleas for justice and deliverance usually end in affirmations of trust in God (Ps. 13). Perhaps the most profound prayer of all is the cry for help when one is overwhelmed by sorrows and pain. And the most dangerous thing one can do at such times is stop communicating openly with God (Ps. 73).[11]

FAITH ALIVE

In what way(s) was your understanding of God's character "momentarily" distorted or your relationship with God adversely affected during a time of loss?

How was that resolved?

What was your greatest source(s) of help in dealing with the suffering? Who most assisted you in the healing and restoration process? How?

CONCLUSION AND CONTINUATION

Verse 22 begins by beautifully and succinctly stating: "So Naomi returned, and Ruth the Moabitess her daughter-in-law with her, who returned from the country of Moab" (v. 22). Thus, it summarizes Ruth and Naomi's activity and invites the reader to mentally recount the remarkable story which has just been heard. Naomi, though describing herself as bitter, expresses true compassion for her daughters-in-law and invokes the name of God on their behalf. Though confounded by the questions which naturally arise from the chaos of compounded tragedies, this old widow of Judah retains a core of faith which enables her to arise and move toward home. Ruth, a Moabitess, willingly leaves her homeland and places her future in the hands of the God of Israel. Instead of recoiling from the stark reality of Noami's financial, emotional, social, and spiritual condition, Ruth clings to Naomi in steadfast personal commitment. In so doing, Ruth's personal commitment becomes a picture of Christ.

Read Philippians 2:4–8 and Galatians 6:2. Describe how Ruth acts like Jesus.

How will the above examples help you to better minister to those suffering grief and loss?

WORD WEALTH

This section concludes with the statement: "Now they came to Bethlehem at the beginning of barley harvest" (v. 22). **Bethlehem** means "House of Bread."[12] For the first time, the author hints that with the beginning of harvest, Bethlehem—which has been the site of famine—will begin to live up to its name.

FAITH ALIVE

Thus, the reader is urged forward and informed that the story has only just begun with the return to Judah. This seed of hope planted at the end of chapter 1 suggests that the love and compassion, faith, and personal commitment revealed in Ruth and Naomi will be woven into a new story of the unfolding acts of God.

What are your expectations and hopes for recovery or reversal in an area of your life? Clearly define them below.

What "seed of hope" has God given you which suggests a new chapter in your story?

Speak your hopes and expectations aloud to God.

1. H. Norman Wright, *So You're Getting Married*, (Ventura: Regal Books, 1985), 10.

2. *Spirit-Filled Life Bible* (Nashville: Thomas Nelson Publishers, 1991), 279, "Word Wealth: Deut. 18:5, name."

3. Ibid., 388, notes on Ruth 1:2, 1:4. Ibid., 388 "Kingdom Dynamics: Ruth 1:1—4:22, Tenacity That Takes the Throne."

4. Ibid., 388, note on Ruth 1:8.

5. Ibid., 391, note on Ruth 3:1.

6. "Moab," *Nelson's Illustrated Bible Dictionary* (Nashville: Thomas Nelson Publishers, 1986).

7. *Spirit-Filled Life Bible*, 389, "Word Wealth: Ruth 1:16, people."

8. Ibid., 389, note on Ruth 1:19

9. Ibid., 389, margin note on Ruth 1:20

10. Ibid., 833, "Word Wealth: Ps. 91:1, Almighty, *shadday.*"

11. "Psalms," *Nelson's Illustrated Bible Dictionary*.

12. *Spirit-Filled Life Bible*, 1324, note on Micah 5:2.

Lesson 3/Gleaning in Boaz's Field: Acting with Initiative and Moral Excellence
(Ruth 2:1–23)

A beautiful account of God's providence in weaving together a love story is recorded in chapter 24 of Genesis. There God attentively hears the prayers of Abraham's servant as he asks for success in finding the right bride for Isaac. The Lord goes before the servant, arranging an amazing chain of events which leaves him filled with wonder and ecstatic with praise for God. In offering an explanation for the events, the servant exclaims "being on the way, the Lord led me . . . " (Gen. 24:27).

Abraham's servant declares the part faith's initiative plays in the providential acts of God's care and favor. But the record of Rebekah's actions further demonstrates the complimentary role of godly character and moral excellence. Certainly this search for a bride could have ended with several different outcomes if either active faith or character were deficient. Only true faith and steadfast commitment to God empower one to initiate in faith or continue in purity without attempting to arrange or manipulate events.

Like the Genesis 24 account, the narrative of Ruth's first day in the fields of Boaz is a record of God's providential care and the beginning of a beautiful love story. In the second chapter of Ruth, the meeting of faith's initiative and moral excellence also brings a full harvest of God's providence and favor.

RUTH'S INITIATIVE, GOD'S PROVIDENCE (2:1-3)

Chapter 2 opens with a narrator's comment which lets the reader know that an important new character is being introduced in this drama of reversals. By stating three times in three verses that Boaz was "of the family of Elimelech" (2:1, twice; 2:3), the author emphasizes the importance of this connection to Naomi's deceased husband and assures that the reader does not miss this fact. Although at least one other person bore this special relationship to Naomi and Ruth, the story will later reveal that Boaz was the widows' only real prospect of both legal and financial help and the recovery of their inheritance in Judah.

What additional information is revealed about Boaz?

 WORD WEALTH

The Hebrew phrase *gibbor havil,* translated **"man of great wealth"** (2:1), has a wider meaning than just economic security. Often rendered "mighty man of valor," it includes the idea of being valiant in war and may thus indicate that Boaz had been a courageous war hero. Additionally, the phrase reflects an elite social class or a "wealth" of power and respect which would place Boaz in high standing within the Bethlehem community. Thus, "man of great wealth" also includes the idea of Boaz's inner qualities. When Boaz later describes Ruth (3:11) using the same Hebrew adjective which describes him here, the adjective is translated "virtuous."[1]

Based on Boaz's question (2:5) and Naomi's exclamation (2:20), what previous knowledge of Boaz did Ruth possess?

What quality of character is seen in Ruth's request? (2:2)

BEHIND THE SCENES

Under the Law, specific provision was made for the poor in Israel. God's heart toward the disadvantaged is succinctly stated in Deuteronomy 10:18. What three categories of people are the focus of His concern there?

Look up the following references, and describe the Law's provision for the poor as it relates to gleaning. (Lev. 19:9, 10; Deut. 24:19)

Do you suppose all landowners were eager to comply with these gleaning laws? How might some "less charitable" landowners respond?

FAITH ALIVE

Read James 1:27. What category of persons mentioned in Deuteronomy 10:18 is missing in this New Testament verse? Why? (See Eph. 2:11–13.)

Based on James 1:27, do you think God's heart has changed toward those suffering unusual hardships? What does this mean to you as a Christian?

How are you personally observing this truth in your everyday life? Within your local church community?

What was Ruth's expectation and hope as she went to glean in the field? (v. 2)

What is surprising about Naomi's consent? In what way(s) does Naomi's reply appear to fall short of the faith seen in Ruth's request? (v. 2)

Describe the act of God's providential care which began the chain of unfolding events. (v. 3)

The way in which the land was farmed made the "happening" of verse 3 more than a mere coincidence.

 BEHIND THE SCENES

Farming in Judah was not like modern farming in the U.S. where a farmer's house is surrounded by his or her land. Houses were collected into villages or cities. All cropland was located outside the city in one large field. Within this field, each person worked the plot bequeathed to him. Simple piles of stones—which were considered sacred landmarks—defined the boundaries of each man's portion or inheritance (See Deut. 19:14).[2] Only one very familiar with the land would know to whom each field belonged.

Boaz's Inquiry and Interest (2:4–7)

With verses 1 through 7, the beginning of the special favor for which Ruth had hoped is seen. As Ruth steps out in faith, she finds herself in a place of blessing.

It has already been noted that Boaz was a man of much wealth. What additional character qualities may be suggested by the greeting he exchanged with his workers? (v. 4; see also Ps. 129:8.)

What may be indicated by the fact that Boaz foregoes an inquiry concerning the harvesting and immediately asks about Ruth (v. 5)?

Boaz's servant gives a summary of Ruth's activities which paints a very positive picture of her character. Although it was not necessary that Ruth ask for that which was her legal right, the servant discloses that Ruth requested permission to glean. He also states that Ruth came to the field early and rested in the field house—or temporary shelter[3]—only a short while. List at least two character strengths which are indicated by Ruth's behavior here (v. 7).

1.

2.

Boaz's Invitation and Blessing (2:8–13)

Certainly in addressing Ruth as "my daughter," (v. 8) Boaz notes the difference in their ages. But much more seems to be involved in this title for Ruth. Boaz's actions reveal a sincere concern to both protect and help Ruth.

What invitation does Boaz extend to Ruth? (vv. 8,9)

BEHIND THE SCENES

The harvest season in an agricultural society such as ancient Bethlehem was a time of joy and hard work. Two major grain harvests were gathered. Barley harvest began in mid-April, and wheat harvest commenced in mid-May.[4] The urgency of the short harvest season required the full effort of every able servant of one's household. Thus, men and women were both involved in reaping the crops and worked close together in the fields. Most likely, male servants cut the stalks and the female servants bound them into bundles to be carried from the field.

Gleaners were not to approach the harvest until the owner's laborers had completed their tasks. Eager gleaners who moved too close to the reapers would be verbally reviled or even physically repulsed. Ruth's position among and behind Boaz's female servants gave her the special advantage of gathering before any other gleaners were allowed near the harvest.[5]

AT A GLANCE

What other special provisions or protections does Boaz offer Ruth in verses 8 and 9? Complete the chart by listing these and the effects each might produce.

SPECIAL PROVISIONS OFFERED BY BOAZ (2:8, 9)		
Provision	Verse	Its Effect
Continuing work in Boaz's field	8	Immediate security; freedom from worry concerning how a foreigner may be received by other landowners.
Working close to Boaz's maid-servants	8, 9	Special protection as though part of Boaz's work force; companionship and inclusion; special position in front of other gleaners.
	9	
	9	

Overwhelmed by Boaz's graciousness, Ruth falls on her face. What character quality does her action and speech reveal?

Why is Ruth especially amazed and appreciative of Boaz's treatment? (v. 10)

In verse 11, Boaz discloses the reason for his special treatment of Ruth. What does Boaz particularly appreciate and respect about Ruth?

What character qualities might one attribute to Ruth based on this report? (v. 11)

Boaz's speech ends with a prayer of blessing for Ruth (v. 12). He asks for Ruth's recompense noting that she had taken refuge under the wings of the Lord God of Israel.

WORD WEALTH

Refuge, *chasah,* means to trust; to hope; to make someone a refuge. This verb is used in Psalm 57:1 to describe David as nestling under God's wing in the same way a small, defenseless baby bird would trustingly hide itself under a parent's feathers. (See: 2 Sam. 22:3; Ps. 91:4; Matt. 23:37.) Psalm 118:8—the middle verse of the Bible—uses this word as it states: "It is better to trust (*chasah*) in the Lord than to put confidence in man."[6]

What do verses 11 and 12 reveal about Boaz's priorities and his character?

Boaz's speech (vv. 11, 12) is the first recorded word of encouragement offered Ruth since her arrival in Bethlehem. Ruth responds to Boaz's words by thanking him. She expresses her appreciation by stating that Boaz had not only comforted her, but spoken "kindly" or straight "to the heart."[7]

Ruth offers the same reason for amazement in verse 13 as she did in verse 10.

WORD WEALTH

"Not like one of your maidservants" (2:13): One, *'echad,* may mean united; unity; one made up of many. Here Ruth states that she is not even one who can rightfully be counted among Boaz's female servants. She emphasizes her status as an alien as lower than that of a maidservant.[8]

FAITH ALIVE

The writer intends for readers to remember that Ruth is a foreigner. This fact is mentioned five times in the first thirteen verses of chapter 2 (vv. 2, 6, 10, 11, 13) and again in verse 21.

What message do you think this emphasis on Ruth's alien status would impart to the first Hebrew readers of the Book of Ruth?

What lesson might modern readers learn concerning God's inclusiveness and favor?

What quality of Ruth's character is seen in verse 13?

PROBING THE DEPTHS

Using your answers from lesson 3 and what you learned about Ruth in lesson 2, compile a list of Ruth's character traits. Do the same for Boaz. Add to these lists as you continue your study of the Book of Ruth. Then answer these questions:

How do these traits compare to the fruit of the Spirit listed in Galatians 5:22, 23; Ephesians 4:2, 3; Colossians 3:12–15; 2 Peter 1:5–7?

Compare Ruth and Boaz's character traits. How might these lists help explain Boaz's interest in and attraction to Ruth (chapters 2, 4) and Ruth's willingness to ask for Boaz's protection (chapter 3)?

Would you consider Ruth and Boaz fit companions for one another? Why?

Boaz's Gift of an Extra Portion (2:14–17)

If Ruth's first day in the barley field had ended with the blessings described in verses 8 through 13, surely she would have recognized God's strong hand of favor. But Boaz's hospitality did not end there. He graciously heaps upon Ruth added portions.

Define the first extra portion given to Ruth and describe how this generous act may have ministered to her (v. 14).

 Behind the Scenes

The midday meal: Although only late morning and evening meals were usually taken, a light midday meal was consumed during harvest to strengthen and refresh the laborers. Not only was it an unusual blessing for Ruth to be invited to eat this meal as one of Boaz's household, but Boaz himself honors Ruth by heaping her plate with grain and handing it to her (v. 14). The "bread" most likely refers to the parched grain— fresh heads of barley lightly roasted over a fire. The "vinegar,"

or sour wine, was traditionally used as a relish to dip parched grain. This sour wine was the refreshing drink received by Jesus on the cross. (See Matt. 27:48; John 19:29,30.)[9]

How did Boaz ensure that Ruth would receive an extra portion for her diligent labor (vv. 15–17)?

 WORD WEALTH

Ephah: a dry measure equal to approximately 22 liters or 5/8 of a bushel. An ephah was an unusually large amount of grain for a single day of gleaning.[10]

RUTH'S TESTIMONY, NAOMI'S TRANSFORMATION (2:18–23)

The last portion of chapter 2 demonstrates the powerful effect of bearing witness to God's activity. When Ruth started out to the field, Naomi offered her no word of encouragement. Rather, the bitterness Naomi confesses in chapter 1 seems to have brought a sense of hopelessness and perhaps even apathy and depression. Yet with Ruth's unfolding testimony, Naomi is not only amazed but transformed. A new confidence in God's ability and willingness to act in covenantal love is stirred within Naomi. She too begins to initiate in faith.

What two material "evidences" of God's favor did Ruth present to Naomi (v. 18)?

Naomi's first responses suggest a rebirth of hope. In what does Naomi hope, and who does she bless (v. 19a)?

As Ruth adds verbal testimony to the evidences of the beginning of reversal (v. 19), Naomi's response moves from hope to faith. What is Naomi's confession, and who does she bless (v. 20)?

How does this confession of faith (v. 13) compare with her earlier statements (1:13, 20, 21)?

What fact affirms the day's events as more than acts of human kindness or coincidence and becomes the catalyst of Naomi's statement of faith (vv. 19b, 20)?

WORD WEALTH

Naomi's exclamation (v. 20) adds to the information concerning Boaz which was offered in verses 1–3. Naomi declares that Boaz is not only "of the family of Elimelech," but "one of our close relatives." Here, **our close relatives,** *goalenu,* may be rendered "our redeemers."[11] When unusual circumstances brought poverty, an Israelite could sell himself, his family, or his land to provide for basic needs (Lev. 25:39–43). The *go'el,* or kinsman-redeemer, was provided to protect the clan from permanent loss of its inheritance (Lev. 25:25). This near relative not only had the first option by law to buy any land sold, he had a strong family obligation to do so (Lev. 25:23–28; Jer. 32:6–10).[12]

How does Naomi evaluate Ruth's disclosure of Boaz's willingness to continue his protection and favor throughout the harvest season? (vv. 21, 22)

WORD WEALTH

Good, *tob,* (v. 22) means right, pleasant, the opposite of sorrow or evil. This same Hebrew word is used in Genesis 1:4 by the Creator to evaluate His product: "God saw the light, that it was good."[13]

What additional character quality may be attributed to Ruth based on her response to Naomi's counsel which is recorded in verse 22 (v. 23)?

 FAITH ALIVE

In the light of the chapter 2 account, what two conditions are necessary to receive both a full harvest of God's providential blessing and human favor?

What help or immediate interventions might you anticipate from God when you move out in faith and act with moral integrity?

Based on this account and the Acts 1:8 explanation of the purpose of the baptism with the Holy Spirit, how important is it that you testify of God's gracious interventions? Why?

Remembering God's acts of intervention and blessing in your own life can neutralize bitterness, re-kindle hope, and renew faith. Begin a journal of your testimonies of God's loving activity in your life. Include special answers to prayer, healings, reversals of circumstances, and words of special comfort and promise spoken to your heart by God during difficult times. When your faith is shaken or some loss pulls you toward bitterness, read these accounts aloud and begin to thank God for His continuing covenantal goodness to you.

1. R. Laird Harris, Gleason L. Archer, Jr., and Bruce K. Waltke, eds., *Theological Wordbook of the Old Testament* (Chicago: Moody Press, 1980), 271–272, no. 624e.

2. *Spirit-Filled Life Bible* (Nashville: Thomas Nelson Publishers, 1991), 390, note on Ruth 2:3.

3. Ibid., 390, note on Ruth 2:7.

4. "Harvest," *Nelson's Illustrated Bible Dictionary* (Nashville: Thomas Nelson Publishers, 1986).

5. Leon Morris, *Ruth: An Introduction and Commentary,* Tyndale Old Testament Commentaries, vol. 7, ed. D.J. Wiseman (Downers Grove: Inter-Varsity Press, 1968), 274–275.

6. *Spirit-Filled Life Bible,* 1354, "Word Wealth: Zeph. 3:12, trust."

7. Ibid., 390, margin note on Ruth 2:13.

8. Ibid., 263, "Word Wealth: Deut. 6:4, one."

9. "Food," "Meals," "Vinegar," *Nelson's Illustrated Bible Dictionary.*

10. "Weights and Measures," *Nelson's Illustrated Bible Dictionary.*

11. *Spirit-Filled Life Bible,* 391, margin note on Ruth 2:20.

12. "Kinsman," *Nelson's Illustrated Bible Dictionary.*

13. *Spirit-Filled Life Bible,* 1205, "Word Wealth: Ezek. 34:14, good."

Lesson 4/Petition at the Threshing Floor: Anticipating Restoration in Quiet Surrender with Patient Trust
(Ruth 3:1–18)

Psalm 62:1 reads: "Truly my soul silently waits for God; from Him comes my salvation."

Of this weighty verse, Maclaren writes: "Literally the words run, 'My soul is silence unto God.' That forcible form of expression describes the completeness of the Psalmist's unmurmuring submission and quiet faith. His whole being is one great stillness, broken by no clamorous passions, by no loud-voiced desires, by no remonstrating reluctance. . . . Here we have the strongest expression of the perfect consent of the whole inward nature in submission and quietness of confidence before God."[1]

Only this kind of surrender to God can resist the tendency to "take control," "make it happen," "do things my way," "stand up for my rights," or "demand justice." Only this type of quiet trust in God allows one to bow to the wisdom of godly counsel and wait without fretting as God in His time brings forth His answer to one's deepest needs. The story recorded in the third chapter of the Book of Ruth is an example of such humble submission and patient trust. It is a shining source of instruction and a challenge to a modern people prone to view aggressive individualism rather than quiet surrender as true strength.

Naomi's Plan (3:1, 2)

It is not clear whether a few days or several weeks elapsed between the day Ruth met Boaz and the events recorded in chapter 3. It is obvious, however, that during the interim, Naomi's hope and faith had been renewed by acts of God's covenant kindness and Ruth's unfailing devotion. Naomi's heart is again moved on Ruth's behalf as during the first moments of the journey back to Bethlehem. Naomi, the compassionate mother-in-law, again voices her concern for her "daughter's" well-being (1:9, 3:1). Her desire is that Ruth exchange the uncertain life of an impoverished laborer for the security of a married wife.

Since Jewish marriages were arranged by parents, Naomi acts in keeping with tradition and her parental role (Gen. 24:3,4; 34:4; Judg. 14:2). Having observed Boaz's generous and protective care of Ruth, Naomi asks (3:2), "Now Boaz, . . . is he not our relative?" Here Naomi suggests a marriage between Boaz and Ruth which would extend Boaz's role of kinsman-redeemer beyond the recovery of Elimelech's land to encompass a levirate marriage to Ruth.

 Bible Extra

Levirate Marriage: The term levirate literally means "husband's brother." Levirate marriage was a form of marriage prescribed by the Law of Moses in which a man was obligated to marry a widow of a brother who died with no male heir. The purpose of this marriage was twofold. First, it was to provide an heir for the dead brother. Thus, the firstborn son of a levirate marriage would bear the name of the deceased brother, thereby preserving both his name and estate. Second, it was the means designed by Law to provide for the continuing welfare of widows. A man who refused to perform this obligation to his deceased brother was called before the city elders. To refuse their admonition brought public shame upon himself and his household (Deut. 25:5–10).[2]

Being a more distant relative than a brother, Boaz was—technically speaking, under no obligation to perform this stipulation of the Law. However, the principle of family commitment illustrated in the levirate marriage and the role of kinsman-redeemer is the basis upon which Naomi makes her suggestion and designs her plan. Naomi looks beyond the letter of the Law and asks Boaz to perform God's heart intent in the Law: "that human loss always be recoverable and that we work with Him in extending such possibilities to those in need."[3]

Naomi goes on to note that both timing and opportunity are appropriate for the presentation of such a petition. She states (3:2b), "In fact, he is winnowing barley tonight at the threshing floor."

BIBLE EXTRA

Winnowing at the Threshing Floor: Winnowing refers to the practice of extracting grain from its surrounding husk. Generally, the outer husk, or chaff, was broken as animals walked over grain spread on the hard surface of the community threshing floor. The resulting grain and husks were then scooped into flat baskets and tossed into the air. A breeze would blow away the lighter chaff and leave the grain.[4] The fact that Boaz was threshing during the evening may indicate that late afternoon and evening winds were the most favorable for the winnowing process.

RUTH'S PREPARATION (3:3–5)

As a newcomer in Bethlehem and a novice concerning the Law and Jewish traditions, Ruth was unskilled in areas of social customs and religious practices. Naomi's perceptive and godly counsel becomes the catalyst which secures Ruth's redemption at the opportune time. Just as Ruth had faithfully followed Naomi's advice in the past (2:22), she again relies on Naomi's godly guidance to inform her of the necessary preparations and protocol. Ruth humbly submits herself to Naomi as her elder and one who is wise in the ways of Israel.

In trusting herself to Naomi's counsel, what does Ruth reveal about her faith in God and her relationship to Him? (vv. 3–5)

What three personal preparations is Ruth instructed to make? (v. 3)

BIBLE EXTRA

The preparations Naomi prescribes for Ruth are those common to Hebrew life. Bathing followed by rubbing the head or entire body with olive oil was a frequent, if not daily, practice associated with personal hygiene (See Deut. 28:40; Matt. 16:16–18). And Naomi's instruction to "put on your best garment" (3:3) may be nothing more than motherly advice to wear a cloak. The Hebrew word used here—which may indicate a variety of ordinary garments—is sometimes translated "mantle."[5] If "mantle" is the appropriate interpretation here, then Naomi was speaking of the typical loose-fitting, one-piece garment which hung below the knees and doubled as a coat and a blanket. Such provision would be necessary when Ruth slept on the threshing floor.[6]

It is also true, however, that these ordinary practices could take on spiritual significance when done as part of the consecration for a sacred task. Bathing, anointing with oil, and donning clean clothes often preceded meeting with and hearing from God and symbolized the seeker's heart purity (See: Gen. 35; Ex. 19:10, 11; Ps. 15; Is. 1:16). Additionally, the anointing Naomi requests may have had special symbolic or prophetic meaning announcing the end of Ruth's widowhood (2 Sam. 14:2; see also Gen. 38:14).

When fully prepared, what procedure is Ruth to follow to inform Boaz of her desire to enter a levirate marriage with him? (v. 4)

FAITH ALIVE

Although Naomi's instruction may have sounded strange or even foolish to Ruth, she commits herself to fully obey Naomi (v. 5). Experiencing a full recovery from life's losses always involves receiving God's counsel with humility and acting in obedience (Pss. 16:7; 73:24). Such counsel means submitting one's will and life to Scripture (Ps. 119:24; 2 Tim. 3:16, 17) and the work of the Holy Spirit (Is. 11:2; John 14:16, 26). It may also entail receiving the guidance of a godly human counselor (Prov. 15:22). God sets persons in leadership in the church who are gifted to edify, comfort and exhort, explain and apply truth, protect and guide the members of the body (Rom. 12:3–8; Cor. 12:1–11, 28; Eph. 4:7–16). Willingness to receive the counsel of those in authority is characteristic of a godly person. Ruth's example shows that God blesses such obedience in ways which exceed all expectations.[7]

Check the items below which are true of your level of submission to God.

Behaviors Which Demonstrate Full Submission to God

____ I daily seek God's presence and guidance through Bible study, prayer, and worship. I consistently take time to listen for the voice of the Spirit.

____ I quickly submit my heart and life to the clear, specific instruction of Scripture. I consciously seek to apply biblical principles to my daily life.

____ Confession of sin, appropriation of Jesus' righteousness, and the anointing of the Holy Spirit mark my daily life.

____ I approach times of special petition with intentional consecration of my will, mind, and life to God.

____ I willingly surrender to God's way of doing things as soon as I am aware of it.

____ When facing a particularly difficult or confusing situation or when my progress toward restoration seems blocked, I am open to seeking the counsel of church leaders or other mature Christians.

____ I believe that God often works through others who may have insight into my situation which I am not able to see on my own. Therefore, I am not offended when asked to obey what may seem menial or simple instruction.

THE PETITION (3:6–9)

Verses 6 and 7 confirm Ruth's full compliance with Naomi's directives, and verses 8 and 9 validate Naomi's wisdom. The response which Naomi had anticipated occurs: Boaz is awakened, giving Ruth an opportunity to identify herself and voice her petition.

WORD WEALTH

"The man was startled" (3:8): The root meaning of the Hebrew verb translated "was startled" is "to shake." The quaking or trembling associated with this word may be induced by physical or emotional causes.[8] Though sometimes associated with fear, it may best be translated in this context as "shivered with cold." Boaz's response make the purpose of uncovering his feet obvious.[9]

Ruth reinforces the symbolism of respectful humility demonstrated by her position at Boaz's feet by identifying herself as "your maidservant" (v. 9). Borrowing a phrase from Boaz's prayer uttered that first day in the field (2:12), Ruth pleads, "Take your maidservant under your wing."

WORD WEALTH

"Take . . . under you wing" (3:9): Although the Hebrew word rendered "wing" is sometimes used literally of a bird's appendage, it is most often used in a figurative and positive sense to refer to God and His protection. Since the word also denotes speed, it is often used in requesting God's refuge or shelter in times of urgent need. Such requests for protection are always founded upon the proven covenant-kindness and trustworthiness of God.[10] (See: "Word Wealth: Refuge," Lesson 3.)

In the context of Ruth 3:9, "take under your wing" may also be translated "spread the corner of your garment over your maidservant." This petition reflects the ancient Middle Eastern practice of casting a garment over one being claimed for marriage. Such a gesture symbolizes both protection and the sharing of provision. Thus, Ruth clearly asks Boaz to marry her based on the kindness, protection, and commitment to family ties which he has already demonstrated.[11]

 ## PROBING THE DEPTHS

To the casual observer looking through twentieth-century eyes, Naomi's directives (3:1–5) and Ruth's ensuing actions (3:6–9) may appear seductive. One must note, however, that Bible narratives do not avoid open disclosure of the sins and flaws of their heroes and heroines. Rather, these accounts often reveal the hidden sins of the heart! Had sexual misconduct taken place at the threshing floor, surely it would have been clearly reported.

On the other hand, the very suggestion of a midnight tryst is inconsistent with both the character of Ruth and Boaz and the spiritual nobility of the book. The actions Naomi prescribes are full of symbolic and cultural meanings which are clearly understood by Boaz (3:10–13). Additionally, it is apparent that Boaz continues to regard Ruth as highly moral and respectable ("virtuous," 3:11; "wealthy," 2:11; Prov. 31:10–28).[12]

Thus, it seems much more reasonable to regard Naomi's instructions as carefully and sensitively designed. It appears that Boaz, although interested, may have been hesitant about approaching Ruth. First, there was an obvious difference in their ages (2:8; 3:10, 11). Second, Boaz's words indicate that not only could Ruth have had her pick among the young men, but this choice is what Boaz expected (3:10). Third, Boaz knew that there was another kinsman who was a closer relative than he (3:12). Naomi's plan provides a private meeting which would avoid undue embarrassment for either Ruth or Boaz. Her arrangement shows that she trusted the impeccable morality of both while at the same time keeping Ruth at a respectable distance which required that Ruth neither touch Boaz nor speak to him first.

Boaz's Response (3:10–13)

Ruth's innermost thoughts and feelings are not revealed in the words of her petition, but she must have felt both a sense of vulnerability and expectancy. Ruth did not have to languish long in these conflicting emotions; Boaz's answer was immediate and clear. He blesses Ruth and assures her of his readiness to act upon her request.

Boaz compares Ruth's former actions (2:20) with her present petition (3:9). He declares her current act of commitment to Naomi a "greater covenant-kindness" (*hesed:* 1:8; 2:20).

What is Boaz's reasoning? (v. 10) How would you evaluate Ruth's act? Why?

What is the basis of Boaz's willingness to comply with Ruth's request? (v. 11)

What double assurance does Boaz offer Ruth (vv. 11–13), and how is his pledge sealed (v. 13)?

Here Boaz shows his respect for the Law and his desire to do things by proper procedure. He also shows his love for Ruth and his deep concern for her welfare when he states, "But if he does not want to perform the duty for you, then I will." (v. 13)

 Word Wealth

The translation of *chafets* (delight) in 3:13 as "does not want" is unfortunate. The verb denotes a strong emotional desire which goes far beyond obligation or the desire to meet a legitimate need. It may mean "cherish" or "love and desire." Here the "object solicits favor by its own intrinsic qualities" so that "the subject is easily attracted to it because it is desirable."[13] Boaz says, "If he does not delight to redeem you because he sees your great worth and cherishes you, then I will redeem you, as the Lord lives!" He prefaces all this by: "And now, my daughter, do not fear."

THE RETURN (3:14–18)

The wait from midnight to pre-dawn must have seemed much longer than the few-hour interim. Boaz had business to attend to in the city, and Ruth's whole life was about to change! When Ruth arose before daybreak, Boaz was already thinking of the details of the day's events.

How does Boaz show that he has assumed the roles of protector and provider for Ruth and Naomi (vv. 14, 15)?

 BEHIND THE SCENES

Ephahs or Seahs? The Hebrew text does not define the six units used to measure the barley Boaz gave to Ruth. It simply states "he measured 6 of barley, and laid it on her" (3:15). The volume of six ephahs would be approximately 3¾ bushels with a weight of 80-90 pounds. Although this was not an unbearable load for a field worker, it seems a heavy load for a female and a great amount to be bundled into a cloak. If measured in seahs (1 seahs=⅓ ephah), the amount would be about 1¼ bushels and weigh closer to 30 pounds. Whatever the exact unit of measure, the load of barley provided a reason for Ruth's presence at the threshing floor. It would be apparent to anyone Ruth met that she had arrived early in order to avoid hard labor during the heat of the day.[14]

When Naomi asked, "How are you" or "How is it with you," Ruth recounted the evening's events (3:16).[15] She emphasized the gift of barley as evidence, or an earnest, of Boaz's intention to fulfill his pledge to them (v. 17). Having heard and seen Ruth's report, Naomi again offers advice.

What is Naomi's last word of counsel (v. 18)?

WORD WEALTH

"Sit still" (3:18), from *yashab* (See: "Word Wealth," Lesson 1, "dwelt") and *hasha,* means to sit down, stay, continue or dwell in silence; to rest quietly in the present place without acting or speaking.[16] Thus, Ruth's final act of surrender to God and trust in His care is to rest in confidence without any clamorous activity. Like the psalmist (Ps. 62:1), her soul is to "wait silently for God" or be "silence unto God." Fully and quietly inhabiting the present means that Ruth must "hold" with patient trust the words and assurance she has received from Boaz (vv. 10–15).

Naomi's advice is based upon her keen perception of Boaz's character. Although Naomi is unable to directly observe Boaz's activity, she knows that he will actively pursue the matter to its end. Naomi states, "the man will not rest until . . . ." Here, Naomi draws a parallel between the character of God and the godly character of Boaz. In the past, God's covenant-kindness had been clearly manifested through Boaz (2:19, 20). Now, just as the God-who-takes-one-under-His-wing acts with speed to provide a refuge and shelter for those who trustingly call out to Him (2:12), so does Boaz (3:9).

BIBLE EXTRA

Since Boaz's introduction in chapter 2, it has become increasingly apparent that in both activity and character, Boaz functions in this biblical account as a picture of God. In chapter 3, Boaz's gracious acceptance of Ruth and his response to her petition is a reflection of God's loving reception of the petitions of His children. Likewise, Ruth functions as an example of the fully surrendered petitioner who receives her request from God.

Boaz's example in Ruth 3:10–13 shows

• God is not offended   Matt 6:8, 9; 7:9–11   (Ruth 3:10)
  when His children
  state their needs.

• God is motivated by a strong "family" commitment to meet the true needs of His children.	Ps. 91:14,15 Rom. 8:31,32	(Ruth 3:11) (Ruth 3:13)
• God highly commends covenant-love as a motivation for petition.	1 John 3:18–23 James 4:3	(Ruth 3:10)

As an exemplary petitioner, Ruth:

• Prepared herself for the act of petitioning	(Ruth 3:3)
• Acted in full obedience to the counsel and wisdom of God with understanding of the principles and intents of God's Law.	(Ruth 3:5–9)
• Made her request (need) known.	(Ruth 3:6,9)
• Heard and believed the words which pledged personal action on her behalf.	(Ruth 3:11) (Ruth 3:13)
• Received and held an "earnest" as assurance of the fulfillment to come.	(Ruth 3:15)
• Rested in quiet assurance as her petition was being answered.	(Ruth 3:18)

 FAITH ALIVE

A. How was Boaz's prayer of 2:12 answered? What principle might be illustrated by this fact?

B. How strongly are you convinced of God's acceptance and willingness to answer your prayers when you approach Him? Are these feelings in line with the Word?

C. Review the principles of petition taken from Ruth's example. Which elements of petitionary prayer are your strengths? Weaknesses? Ask the Holy Spirit to help you become more effective in your prayer life as you begin applying these principles.

1. Alexander Maclaren, *Expositions of Holy Scripture* (Grand Rapids: Wm. B. Eerdmans Publishing Co., 1932), 67.

2. "Levirate Marriage," *Nelson's Illustrated Bible Dictionary* (Nashville: Thomas Nelson Publishers, 1986).

3. *Spirit-Filled Life Bible* (Nashville: Thomas Nelson Publishers, 1991), 387, "Ruth: Introduction, Personal Application."

4. Ibid., 391, note on Ruth 3:2.

5. R. Laird Harris, Gleason L. Archer, Jr., and Bruce K. Waltke, eds., *Theological Wordbook of the Old Testament* (Chicago: Moody Press, 1980), 879, no. 2270a.

6. "Dress of the Bible," *Nelson's Illustrated Bible Dictionary.*

7. *Spirit-Filled Life Bible*, 394, "Ruth: Truth in Action, Keys to Relating to Authority."

8. *Theological Wordbook of the Old Testament*, 321–322, no 735.

9. *Spirit-Filled Life Bible*, 391, note on Ruth 3:7, 8.

10. *Theological Wordbook of the Old Testament*, 446–447, no. 1003a.

11. *Spirit-Filled Life Bible*, 391–392, note on Ruth 3:9.

12. Ibid., 391-392, notes on Ruth 3:3—5 and Ruth 3:9.

13. *Theological Wordbook of the Old Testament.* 310-311, no. 712. *Spirit-Filled Life Bible*, 852, "Word Wealth: Ps. 112:1, delights."

Lesson 5/Love's Transaction at the City Gate: Images of Our Redeemer
(Ruth 4:1–12)

It has been twenty years since I first heard the story of the wealthy bachelor who astounded all the people of his islands with his unusual negotiations to obtain a bride. When a bride was selected, it was customary for the prospective groom to sit down with the young woman's father in the presence of the island's elders to decide upon a purchase price. Each father attempted to get the highest price possible for the loss of his daughter, and each future husband attempted obtain a good deal.

But this young man—instead of working to lower the father's asking price—continued to raise the father's bid until he reached the unheard-of price of eight healthy cows! For months, the islands' populace buzzed with the news as the amazed people recounted the story of Johnny Lingo's transaction. From generation to generation, the story was handed down, for never before nor after had a man of these islands so delighted in his bride as to pay such a high price!

So also is the story of Boaz's love for Ruth. Though the widow's nearest of kin lives in anonymity, Boaz is remembered well in the pages of Hebrew history. His generous love was willing to pay the price that others would not or could not pay for he so delighted to redeem his bride. Yet Boaz's redeeming love for Ruth is just a shadow of the greatest love known to humankind. Jesus, our Great Redeemer, made himself a kinsman by willingly leaving the splendor of His glory and becoming flesh. When there was no intercessor to be found who could pay our sin-debt, He took upon Himself the whole debt. Becoming a curse for us, He died a sinner's death and arose in victory releasing us from all death and sin-curse. And it was all for love's sake.

PRELIMINARIES AT THE CITY GATE (4:1, 2)

The opening sentence of chapter 4 suggests Boaz's immediate action concerning Ruth's redemption. In fact, verse 15 chapter 3, of the traditional Hebrew Old Testament (the Masoretic Text) uses the masculine indicating "he (not *she*) left for the city" as soon as the bundle of grain was placed on Ruth.[1] Just as Ruth's love and commitment to Naomi had urged her to initiate in faith (2:2, 3), so Boaz moved forward in confidence. Upon arrival in Bethlehem, Boaz sat down at the city gate (4:1).

BEHIND THE SCENES

The city gate (4:1) technically refers to a massive wooden door in the city wall through which all traffic passed. This gate was generally opened during the day for commerce and closed at night for safety. The phrase, however, may also refer to the area just inside the gate which functioned somewhat like an early American town square or the small-town court-squares of a century or two ago. Here, people met to talk, and vendors' goods were bought and sold. It was also at the gate that important legal matters were discussed and settled (See: 2 Sam. 15:2; 1 Kin. 22:10). Thus, "gates" came to symbolize power and authority.[2]

Like Ruth, Boaz's initiation is met by God's providential activity. What words in this section parallel "and she happened to . . ." of Ruth 2:3? (v. 1)

To "sit down" at the city gate implied an intentional business or legal purpose. Who does Boaz ask to join him in this activity? (vv. 1, 2)

WORD WEALTH

Boaz's friend and the ten elders (4:1, 2) Here, "friend," *peloni almoni,* may be translated literally as "so and so" indicating a specific, albeit anonymous, person.[3] Thus, the nearest kinsman's name appears to be intentionally left out of this account. It is likely that the writer is subtly stating by this absence that the close relative's name was not worthy of mention in comparison to Boaz's.

"Elders," or those of "old age," were chosen by Moses as leaders of the groups which made up Israel. With the settling of the Promised Land, bodies of elders ruled each city. These elders "sat" to confirm legal transactions and functioned much like contemporary judges in civil affairs.[4] Boaz's designation of ten elders may indicate the number needed for the legal transaction of redemption. Although the leading-elders here are men, their function and authority was not exclusively limited to the male gender. Deborah, a deliverer and prophetess, also "sat" authoritatively during this time period to judge among the people and decide matters of the Law. (See: Judg. 4:4, 5).

LOVE'S SURE TRANSACTION

Boaz's love for Ruth and his concern for the two widows is made evident by the way in which he conducts the redemption process. Boaz skillfully orders his conversation with the close relative, playing his "trumpcard" last. In this way, if the kinsman is able to bear the financial cost of redemption, Boaz can still test his heart. Boaz had promised Ruth: "If he does not want to perform the duty for you, then I will" (3:13), and Boaz is determined to keep his pledge!

What topic does Boaz address first? What does he ask the close relative to do? (vv. 3, 4)

Read Leviticus 25:23–25. What principle stands behind redemption of the land?

"To inform you" (v. 4) literally means "to uncover your ear."[5] Based on this word picture and the community reports of 1:19 and 2:11, what seems to be the nearest relative's attitude toward Naomi and his level of concern for her welfare?

In verse 4, Boaz pushes the kinsman to make a prompt decision. Why might the close relative feel pressured to purchase the land? How does Boaz attempt to lead him away from this pressure? (v. 4)

PROBING THE DEPTHS

Just how many people left their conversations and the vendors' wares to border the circle of elders is unknown (vv. 4, 9, 11). Surely Boaz's kindness to the Moabite widow and her mother-in-law must have been nearly as well reported around Bethlehem as Ruth's first covenant-kindnesses. And Boaz's knowledge of Naomi's situation (v. 3) certainly suggests a broader contact between the widows and Boaz during the weeks of harvest than the few recorded events.

It seems that Boaz's growing affection for Ruth would have been difficult to conceal in this close-knit community. More than a few sitting by must have suspected Boaz's intentions. Not only was redemption of land not an everyday occurrence, the "something more" which might be involved here would have created quite a stir! Surely, such news about wealthy and prominent Boaz and the Moabitess quickly spread among those at the gate and drew an increasing gathering as the transaction progressed.

The surprised reader can almost hear the crowd's gasp as the close relative agrees to pay the redemption price for the land. But Boaz continues on, seemingly undaunted. What is Boaz's "trumpcard"—his most powerful move to overturn the relative's purchase? (v. 5)

How might this second requirement test the close relative's motives for the redemption?

 BEHIND THE SCENES

The mention of Ruth adds further legal conditions to the redemption. If the close relative must only pay Naomi the purchase price, he would be out some money. His own family inheritance would be somewhat diminished. But he would eventually get a return on his investment. Since Naomi was too old to bear an heir to Elimelech, the land would revert to the closest relative at her death and become part of his family's inheritance (Num. 27:8-11). With Ruth as an added factor, the kinsman would have to pay the purchase price of the land, marry Ruth and support her, then give up any rights to the land when an heir was born from her. The close relative might even entangle his own family inheritance if Ruth's first son was the only male heir. This redemption would be costly, and there would be no financial advantage to such an arrangement. To act as kinsman-redeemer in the fullest sense would require sacrificial covenant-love and a true desire to build up another's house.

How does the closest relative answer in light of this additional requirement? Why? (v. 6)

How does the *peloni almoni* indicate the surrender of his right to redeem the land and marry Ruth? (vv. 7, 8)

Love's Announcement (4:9, 10)

The close-lipped reporting of Boaz's announcement makes the reader want to voice the victory shout which Boaz conceals with his dignified manner. Surely, his words must have been strong and clear, his eye contact direct and forceful, reflecting his strong commitment and the love and pride he felt for Ruth.

Boaz calls upon the elders and all the people, reminding them of their status as legal witnesses. What does Boaz declare as his purchase? And from whom does he buy? (v. 9)

Whether there were other debts owed which Boaz redeems is not known, but he clearly retrieves **on this day** by purchase all the lost inheritance of Elimelech's family. What is his "acquisition"? In what two ways will Elimelech's family be further enhanced **in the future** by Boaz's redemptive activity? (v. 10)

WORD WEALTH

Words related to redemption are used fifteen times in verses 4 through 10. **Redeemed** *(ga'al)*, means ransom, repurchase, to set free by avenging or repaying. The Hebrew word refers to buying back something a person lost through helplessness, poverty, or violence. Furthermore, the one who does the redeeming is often a close relative who is in a stronger position and thus buys back the lost property on behalf of his weaker relative. Here, Boaz is a redeemer (vv. 9, 10). But Psalm 72:14 points forward to Messiah as the Redeemer stating, "He will redeem *(ga'al)* their life [of the needy] from oppression and violence."[6]

FAITH ALIVE

Jesus Our Redeemer

Because of His great love for humanity, God made Himself our kinsman by becoming flesh (John 1:14; Heb. 2:14, 17). When we—as individuals and the human race—were without strength to release ourselves from sin's sickness and death and restore our relationship with God, Jesus did what we could not do for ourselves (Ps. 49:7–9, 15; Rom. 3:23–25; 5:6, 12). He offered His sinless life pouring out His blood as the only adequate ransom for us (Eph. 1:7, 1 Pet. 1:18, 19). He restored our family name and inheritance making all who believe in Him both children of God and heirs (John 1:12, 13; 1 Tim. 2:5, 6).

In one transaction (Jesus' death and resurrection), Jesus retrieved all our lost inheritance (Heb. 9:15). Yet, this redemptive act has implications for both the present and the future. Now, all who receive Jesus as Savior are released from sin's penalty and are no longer slaves to sin (Rom. 5:18, 19; 6:10–18; Col. 2:13, 14). In addition, all we who are reunited with God through Jesus' redeeming work eagerly await the inheritance which is kept for us: eternal life, the full redemption of our bodies, and the release of the whole creation (Rom. 8:23; Heb. 10:12–13; 1 Pet. 1:4, 5).

What does Boaz declare as the role of those who have seen and heard love's transaction? (vv. 9, 10).

How are you bearing witness to Jesus' redemptive work?

Use the facts from the paragraphs above to list at least five appropriate responses to our Redeemer's gift of love.

THE PRONOUNCEMENT OF BLESSING (4:11, 12)

The people and elders answer Boaz's call to witness by heartily confirming the extraordinary action which has taken place before them (v. 11). Hardly have the words of legal validation escaped their lips before enthusiastic words of blessing pour out upon Boaz and his bride. The elders direct their blessing first to Ruth, then to Boaz, then the household which they will establish together (vv. 11, 12).

Why do you think the elders might picture Ruth's blessed state as similar to both Rachel and Leah? (v. 11; See: Gen. 29:18, 31–35)

WORD WEALTH

Built, *banah,* may mean constructed, founded, set up, or obtained children. It is thought that *banah* is the root of both "son" (*ben*) and "children" (*banim*). In Psalm 102:16, the Lord's building of Zion is connected with the manifestation of His glory. Contrary to much twentieth-century thought, Scripture states that children are a blessing from the Lord, a gift both to their parents and to the congregation of Israel (Gen. 1:28; Ps. 127:3–5).[7]

What two blessings do the elders ask for Boaz? (v. 11)

WORD WEALTH

Prosper and be famous (4:11): Given the equivalent names of Bethlehem and Ephrathah (Gen. 35:18), a parallelism may be intended to make emphatic this word of blessing. The "might" or "prosperity" (*chayil*: See "Word Wealth," Lesson 3) requested would enlarge the wealth, character, and fame Boaz has already attained (2:1). Paired with "be of name" (from *shem*; See "Word Wealth," Lesson 2), it asks that Boaz be especially increased by a renowned family lineage.

This prayer requests many sons be born to Boaz that his name as well as Mahlon's be strong in Bethlehem.

What is the main emphasis of the elders' blessing upon the house of Ruth and Boaz (v. 12)?

 BIBLE EXTRA

The house of Perez (4:12): In asking that Boaz's house be like that of Perez, the elders' prayer encompasses both the blessing and prophecy given over Judah and a prominent place in that blessing. When Moses took the first census of Israel, not only did the tribe of Judah possess the largest army among the twelve tribes, but a descendant of Perez stood at the head of the tribe of Judah (Num. 1:4, 7; 2:3).

Read Genesis 49:8–13, which records Jacob's blessing and prophecy concerning Judah's descendants. What position were descendants of Judah to occupy in the nation of Israel? How long?

Now read Genesis 38, which gives the unusual background of Perez's conception and birth. What similarities are there between Tamar's and Ruth's stories? In what way are their stories very different?

When no redeemer could be found for Tamar, God worked a reversal for her and caused her offspring to rise to prominence. What does Tamar's story tell you about God?

WORD WEALTH

Perez (4:12), *perets*, means breach or breakthrough. At Perez's birth the midwife exclaimed, "How have you broken a break for yourself?" His story is one of reversal, for Perez won the inheritance of the firstborn son by "breaking through" in front of his twin brother and reversing the birth order (Gen. 38:29; See also Num. 26:20 where his name is listed first).[8]

The words spoken by the elders of Boaz's people (4:4, 11, 12) may have been traditional words of congratulations spoken over all descendants of Perez when they married. But, then as now, it is much easier to sincerely and heartily congratulate some couples than others!

FAITH ALIVE

Could you offer heartfelt congratulations to a couple like Boaz and Ruth? Why?

Do you think Boaz will be a "covenant-keeper"? How about Ruth? What is the basis of your evaluation?

Could you honestly be called a "covenant-keeper"?

One's level of commitment to God and the ability to faithfully and joyfully keep covenant in marriage are directly related. Second Chronicles 16:9 states: "For the eyes of the Lord range throughout the earth, to strengthen those whose hearts are fully committed to him."[9] The Spirit of God actually "makes strong" or "causes to prevail" those whose hearts are "perfect" toward Him.[10]

Take time to commit yourself anew to God. Thank God for His Holy Spirit and His eagerness to empower His fully-committed people. Ask God to make you a strong covenant-keeper in your marriage relationship, your relationships with family and friends, and your relationship to the local church.

1. *Spirit-Filled Life Bible* (Nashville: Thomas Nelson Publishers, 1991), 392, margin note on Ruth 3:15.

2. "Gate, City," *Nelson's Illustrated Bible Dictionary* (Nashville: Thomas Nelson Publishers, 1986).

3. *Spirit-Filled Life Bible*, 392, margin note on Ruth 4:1.

4. "Elder," *Nelson's Illustrated Bible Dictionary, Spirit-Filled Life Bible*, 392, note on Ruth 4:2.

5. *Spirit-Filled Life Bible*, 392, margin note on Ruth 4:4.

6. Ibid., 1031, "Word Wealth: Is. 52:9, redeemed."

7. Ibid., 1366, "Word Wealth: Zech. 1:16, built."

8. Ibid., 1186, "Word Wealth: Ezek. 22:30, gap."

9. *The NIV Topical Study Bible* (Grand Rapids: Zondervan Bible Publishers, 1980).

10. R. Laird Harris, Gleason L. Archer, Jr., and Bruce K. Waltke, eds., *Theological Wordbook of the Old Testament* (Chicago: Moody Press, 1980), 276, 930–931, nos. 636 and 2401.

Lesson 6/Reversal at Bethlehem: Images of Restoration

(Ruth 4:13–22)

Because you are my help,
I sing in the shadow of your wings.
My soul clings to you;
Your right hand upholds me.
Psalm 63:7.8 NIV [1]

Here the psalmist pictures himself as a tiny bird enveloped in the comfort and protection of the wing of the One in whom he completely trusts. He is full and warm; he has feasted and is satisfied. His soul overflows with health, and he rests upon the generous blessings of God. His heart is united to his Protector in mutual love. Out of this overflowing abundance and well-being, he throws back his head and sings with complete abandon: "Your lovingkindness is better than life!" He passionately declares, "My lips shall praise you, and I will bless you with uplifted hands!" (Ps. 63:3, 4, 5).

Surely, these words could describe the heart-song of all the main characters of the little Book of Ruth as they begin to see clearly God's hand in restoration. The conclusion of chapter 4 reveals the ways in which each one—Naomi, Ruth, and Boaz—personally experienced God's overflowing goodness in a great reversal. It also shows how God graciously wove their individual stories into the Great Story of His acts.

Their stories become an encouragement and source of hope for all who trust in the Redeemer. Like the psalmist, the three experienced the truth that even in the desert places of life when God's hand of blessing and care is difficult to see, God is still at work. No trial or crisis, no great calamity or terror of chaos is so great that it cannot be transformed in His hand.

Just as Boaz prayed, the Lord recompenses our labors of faithful and committed love and rewards all who run under His wing for refuge (2:12). Like Naomi, Ruth, and Boaz, we may not comprehend the full scope of God's intervention in this lifetime (4:18–22). But we can know that when we ask in full surrender and trust, He always spreads His wing over us. When we come to see all things from under that wing, the desert and the inscrutable darknesses of life fade and become to us also a place of singing and a promise of restoration.

RUTH'S REVERSAL AND BOAZ'S RESTORATION (4:13)

Readers of Ruth may wish that the author had added some words to describe the love and joy of these newlyweds who were likely the talk of the town. The writer accounts for the first year of Ruth and Boaz's marriage with a few words which yield only the bare-bones facts. But then, what is given is really all that is needed. Ruth and Boaz have both proven by their previous actions that they understand that love is an active commitment which continually seeks another's good (see 1 Cor. 13). Readers may confidently conclude that their marriage brought rest and joy.

Boaz kept his commitment and with delight took Ruth as his wife. God likewise demonstrated His faithfulness. What was God's special intervention on Ruth's behalf? (v. 13)

    WORD WEALTH

"The Lord gave her conception" (4:13) implies a miracle on Ruth's behalf. Not only does the wording of verse thirteen suggest an immediacy to the act of conception, the announcement overturns the barrenness of the ten years in which Ruth was married to Mahlon (1:4, 5). In the Old Testament, barrenness was considered a curse. Women who could not conceive and bear children not only felt personal shame, but at times suffered public humiliation at the hands of others. Scripture shows that God opens and closes the womb. Several leading women described in the Old Testament as barren experienced miraculous births by God's intervention (See: Gen. 11:30; 25:21; 29:31; Judg. 13:2, 3; 1 Sam. 2:5).[2]

Through the birth of this first son, God showed His faithfulness to Boaz in a surprising way. Read Ruth 4:21, Matthew 1:5, and Luke 3:32. What unexpected "restoration" did this kinsman-redeemer experience?

AT A GLANCE

Ruth personally experienced multiple reversals which may be inferred from the facts of verse 13.

Ruth's Personal Restoration (4:13)	
Moabitess (outsider) ----➤	wife of a Bethlehemite; as a mother in Judah, her offspring would give her a permanent place within the community and genealogy of Israel.
Poverty-stricken --------➤ laborer	finds rest from hard labor and abundance in the home of her prominent and wealthy husband
Widow --------------➤	beloved wife redeemed at a high price
Barren --------------➤	fruitful

FAITH ALIVE

Were Ruth's reversals direct answers to prayer? Read the prayer(s) contained in the references beside each name. Then list Ruth's reversals(s) which could be attributed to each petition.

Possible Direct Answers to Prayer		
Person	Reference	Ruth's Reversals Attributable to Answered Prayer
Naomi	1:8; 3:1	
Ruth	2:2	
Boaz	2:12	
Elders	4:11, 12	

What have you learned from reading the prayers and completing the tables above?

How will your prayer life change as a result?

NAOMI'S GREAT REVERSAL (4:14–17)

This section probably describes the day of the formal presentation of Ruth and Boaz's son (Lev. 12). Much like the presentation and naming of John the Baptist (Luke 1:58–66), relatives and neighbors have gathered for the joyful occasion. However, the author's focus here is not on the child as one would expect. Likewise, Ruth receives only indirect mention, and Boaz is not named at all.

Just as Naomi's losses have been those most prominently noted, Naomi's reversal is now the main focus of restoration activity. Thus, the women gathered at the presentation of Ruth's son rejoice over God's goodness to Naomi. What has God given Naomi **this day**? And to whom do the women refer when using this title? (v. 14)

Although Boaz redeemed the land for Naomi, only a male heir can continue to hold the land for Elimelech's family. By producing other male heirs, this son will extend Mahlon's family name and the claim to Elimelech's estate. Thus, the blessing the women spoke for the child is almost identical to the personal blessing the elders gave to Boaz in anticipation of his marriage to Ruth (v. 11).

In what way is the child's blessing different from Boaz's? (vv. 11, 14)

How was this blessing fulfilled? (v. 17)

In what way(s) will this son function as a "greater *go'el*" (redeemer) than Boaz? (v. 15)

WORD WEALTH

A restorer of life (4:15): "Restorer," *shub*, means to turn back, turn, return, restore, retrieve, reverse. Its usual sense is "return," that is, to go back to the point of departure. In a spiritual sense, it can indicate either a turning away from God or a turning away from sin and toward God. As a restorer of life, the child would bring a full reversal of circumstances which would retrieve Naomi's former position and way of life.[3]

Turn back to Lesson 1 and review the charts you completed entitled: "The Beginning of Naomi's Sorrows (1:1, 2)" and "Naomi's Years of Sorrow in Moab (1:3–5)." Put a checkmark in front of each loss which has been reversed for Naomi through the birth of this child.

WORD WEALTH

Nourisher of old age (4:15): "Nourisher," *chul,* means to sustain, maintain, provide food, hold up, protect, support, defend, to supply the means necessary for living. The primary meaning of *chul* is "to measure out a provision of food." In

Naomi's old age, she will not have to worry even if Boaz dies before her. This "son" will provide the daily portion she requires for life.[4]

Read verses 16 and 17. How might this grandchild be to Naomi a "nourisher of old age" in an emotional and spiritual sense?

In chapter 1, verses 20 and 21, Naomi described herself as "bitter," "empty," and "afflicted by the Almighty." Surely, holding her grandson brought Naomi joy, filled her empty arms, and caused her to see God's loving-kindness. But who do the women credit as the true human instrument of restoration? (v. 15) Do you agree with their evaluation? Why?

Why might the women of the neighborhood name the child Obed, or "Servant,"[5] if he is considered a "son" to Naomi? (v. 17)

How might "Servant" be an appropriate name for a child born of Ruth and Boaz's union?

REVERSAL AT BETHLEHEM (4:18–22)

The ending of the Book of Ruth may at first seem strange, awkward, or even out of place to modern readers. The fact that Ruth ends with a genealogy lends strong support to the proposition that the primary purpose for writing the Book of Ruth was to provide a historical base for the family background of David, from whom the Messiah-Redeemer would come.[6] And the book's placement in the Old Testament after the Book of Judges and before the accounts of the kings makes the final genealogy logical.

Yet, the genealogy is also quite appropriate for other reasons. The Book of Ruth may, in one sense, be a contrast, counterpoint, or commentary against the Book of Judges itself. During a time of situational ethics, shallow commitments, unstable and diffuse government, one man named Boaz and one Moabitess named Ruth yielded the government of their lives fully to God. Their lives illustrate the value of proper priorities and faithful commitment which is built upon steadfast trust in God. Their story shows that one life can make a difference. Like a pebble thrown into the pool of Israel, the faithful lives of two people affected generations to come—a family and clan, a city, a nation, and the world.

Review lessons 2 through 4 by listing the two main character traits noted in each lesson heading. (Although the main focus was on Ruth's character, these same traits were equally seen in Boaz.)

Lesson 2: _____

_____

Lesson 3: _____

_____

Lesson 4: _____

_____

BIBLE EXTRA

Trace the influence of the godly character and lives of Ruth and Boaz by reading the Scripture references and recording the effect of their lives upon the following:

Family and Clan: Fill in the blanks.

Ruth 4:17	Obed was "Servant"_____
Acts 13:22	David was _____
Luke 2:4, 5	Their descendants_____ and _____
Is. 42:1–4,	were honored to bear and provide the care
52:13	and training for Jesus who was Himself called

_____.

City of Bethlehem: Describe the fame brought to Bethlehem because of Ruth and Boaz's descendants.

1 Samuel 16:1, 13

1 Samuel 17:12

Micah 5:2

Matthew 2:1; Luke 2:11

Nation of Israel: Describe the ways in which the nation was blessed through Ruth and Boaz's descendants.

2 Samuel 2:4, 5:1–3

1 Kings 15:3; 2 Chronicles 17:3; 29:1, 2

Matthew 1:1

Humanity: How was the world blessed through the "Greater David" born of Mary and conceived of the Holy Spirit?

Matthew 2:21, 29–32

Read Ruth 4:18–20 again. Then read Matthew 1:1–17. What message may be intended by the inclusion of Tamar, Rahab (a Gentile), and Ruth in the genealogy of Jesus?

 FAITH ALIVE

Ruth and Boaz could not have known how God would use their faithful lives in His plan. They did understand that their submission to God and commitment to family could bring restoration to at least one life. How does their example speak to you personally? What will you do in light of that? Write your commitments below.

What have you learned about God from this study of the Book of Ruth? Briefly list those concepts below.

How have you been strengthened or changed during the course of this study? Take time to thank God for His Word and the power of the Holy Spirit.

Scan your answers to the "Faith Alive" sections of the previous lessons. What areas of personal and spiritual growth targeted by the Holy Spirit need further attention? What is your growth plan for each of these areas?

1. *The NIV Topical Study Bible* (Grand Rapids: Zondervan Bible Publishers, 1989).
2. "Barren," *Nelson's Illustrated Bible Dictionary* (Nashville: Thomas Nelson Publishers, 1986).
3. *Spirit-Filled Life Bible* (Nashville: Thomas Nelson Publishers, 1991), 393, "Word Wealth: Ruth 4:15, restorer."
4. Ibid., 801, "Word Wealth: Ps. 55:22, sustain."
5. Ibid., 393, note on Ruth 4:17.
6. Ibid., 393, note on Ruth 4:18–22.

Lesson 7/The Opening of Opportunity
(Esther 1:1—2:4)

No life has ever been so attuned to the presence of opportunity as that of our Lord Jesus Christ. Wherever Jesus went, He never missed a thing—not a facial expression, not a need, not an open heart, or a buried thought. The Samaritan at the well, the child outside the circle of the disciples, the woman among the throng who touched His garment—all these "appointments" He greedily seized for the Kingdom of God.

Jesus knew what we must learn: Each day is spiked with opportunity. Auspicious moments pepper the normal course of events or appear suddenly as windows in previously closed or opposing circumstances.[1] Each of these opportunities holds the possibility to affect, powerfully influence, or dramatically change the direction of one's own life and the lives of many others.

The Book of Esther shows that opportunity wisely used for God's purposes can reverse the course of events of an entire people. In this study we will look at the opportunities of: cooperating with God's plan (lesson 8), announcing our allegiance (lesson 9), identifying with the distressed (lesson 10), moving with the Spirit (lesson 11), securing full petition (lesson 12), and maintaining victory (lesson 13). We will find that not all opportunities are easy to recognize. Some come as points of crises; others come disguised in the routine of the day. Some come at times of great personal favor and advancement; still others are buried in adverse circumstances. But each opportunity is an opening to be grasped for the kingdom of God. *Carpe diem!*

THE BOOK OF ESTHER

The Old Testament Book of Esther is placed in the English Bible with the books of the history of the nation Israel.

It follows Ezra and Nehemiah, which also describe events during the rule of Persia. While Ezra and Nehemiah deal with return of the Jewish people from captivity in Babylon and the rebuilding of Jerusalem, Esther is an account of the Jews who remained in the land of exile. The Book of Esther shows how God preserves His "nation" even when dispersed among a hostile Gentile people. (See "Books About the History of Israel" in lesson 1.)

 AT A GLANCE

The Times of Ezra, Nehemiah, and Esther[2]	
Events of the Book of Esther (483–471 B.C.)	**Events of the Book of Nehemiah** (445–ca. 425 B.C.)
├─────────┤	├─────┤
550 525 500 475 450 425 400	
├ **Events of the Book of Ezra** ┤ (538–458 B.C.)	
Zerubbabel and first return of exiles: Ezra 1—6 (538 B.C.)	Ezra and second return of exiles: Ezra 7—10 (458 B.C.)

Facts About the Book of Esther
Author: Based on the wide knowledge of Persian life demonstrated in the writing, Esther was likely authored by a Persian Jew. Although Mordecai or Ezra have been suggested as the writer, the author remains unknown.
Date: Esther 10:2 implies that King Ahasuerus's reign had ended. Thus, the book of Esther was probably written shortly after 465 B.C.
Key Verses: Key to the book's message: Esther 4:14 Most quoted verse: Esther 4:16 "If I perish, I perish."
Unique Feature: God's name is not mentioned even once. However God's hand is clearly seen in the ordering of events and in His work through both Esther and Mordecai.[3]

The first section of the Book of Esther (1:1—2:4) seems to be written almost as a farce—"a satirical comedy which utilizes exaggerated or ridiculous situations and plots."[4] In the first few verses, the king of Persia appears to be a powerful ruler. Yet, the further one reads in the opening section, the more evident it becomes that this "powerful ruler" is ruled by his own self-indulgence and pitiful lack of wisdom. Several character flaws negate the ability of this Gentile king to make wise use of the opportunity afforded by his position and authority. He and his advisors are caricatures of "the great depth and mighty expanse" of human wisdom and power which is not yielded to God and sensitive to His precepts.

THE KING'S FEASTS (1:1–9)

The first verses of Esther reveal the massive extent of King Ahasuerus's political power and his great wealth. Like the behind-the-scene stories of the rich and famous, these verses offer an inside look at a lifestyle of pomp and extravagance difficult for most people to imagine.

Who is Ahasuerus? (Esth. 1:1; Ezra 4:6) When and where do the opening events occur? (Esth. 1:1–3)

 AT A GLANCE

Persian Kings of the Restoration, 559–404 B.C.[5]							
				Xerxes I			
Cyrus	Cambyses	Smerdis	Darius I	(Ahasuerus)	Artaxerxes I	Xerxes II	Darius II
559–530	530–522	522	522–486	(486–465)	465–424	424	423–404
575	550	525	500	475	450	425	400

 BEHIND THE SCENES

Ahasuerus, also known by his Greek name Xerxes I, was a king of Persia who ruled from 485 to 464 B.C. He succeeded his father Darius Hystatpis, who had quelled rebellion in the far regions of the kingdom and unified the huge Persian Empire by developing state highways, a postal system, and standard coinage, weights, and measures. Like his father Darius, Ahasuerus attempted to conquer the Greeks and further extend the Persian Empire, but was unsuccessful. (Ahasuerus' last attempt to oust the Greeks probably occurred between the events recorded in chapter 1 and the event which opens chapter 2)[6]

Ahasuerus reigned over more than 20 satraps, or 127 provinces, from India (area drained by the Indus River or modern Pakistan) to Ethiopia (the area south of Egypt or modern northern Sudan). He made Shushan (Susa) his citadel. This fortified palace complex was elevated 120 feet above the rest of the city of Shushan for the king's exaltation and protection. Much of the opulence of Ahasuerus' palace described in chapter 1 has been verified by archaeological excavation of Xerxes' palace.

Described as bold and ambitious in war, Ahasuerus was also noted for his self-indulgence and rage. When his brother's wife refused his sexual advances, Ahasuerus seduced her daughter and then arranged the murder of the entire family.[7]

Who were the key people invited to Ahasuerus's first feast? (1:3)

What was the stated purpose of the six months of banqueting? (1:3, 4) What deeper purpose might be behind a banquet for this particular group?

BEHIND THE SCENES

Media (1:3), the ancient name for modern northwest Iran, was the most important province of Persia. It was politically and militarily wise to develop and maintain the allegiance of Media. Thus, many customs and laws of the Medes were incorporated by Persia, and many leading Medes were given high positions in the Persian Empire.[8]

Who made the guest list for the shorter feast? (1:5, 9) How might this action also be a "politically correct" move? A pompous move? (1:7, 8)

What adjectives best describe Ahasuerus's seven-day feast which concluded the 180-day banquet and display? (1:5–8)

According to Ecclesiastes 10:16–18, what did Ahasuerus really show by this excessive display and consumption? (1:2-9)

What two moral flaws seem to dominate Ahasuerus's activity recorded in Esther 1:1–9?

THE KING'S FOLLY (1:10–13)

The king's grand display did not end with sumptuous feasting, the showy presentation of his wealth, or the week of unbridled drinking. Ahasuerus decides to show his greatness by displaying the queen's beauty.

 WORD WEALTH

Beauty (1:11), *yophi,* means splendor, brightness, fairness; perfect in physical form; flawless in symmetry.[9] Women who have had their value gauged solely by physical beauty can understand the offensiveness of Ahasuerus's command. Proverbs 31:30, 31 states that physical beauty is fleeting. Women are to be praised and admired for their fear of God and their good works inside and outside the home.

How did the king's plan to further inflate his image backfire? (1:10–13)

What does the king's fury show about his relationship to Vashti and the way in which he viewed her? (v. 13)

Given the little we know about the situation, do you think Vashti's refusal was right or wrong? Why? (vv. 10, 13)

What alternatives did Vashti have? Is there some way she could maintain her dignity and protect the king's reputation?

FAITH ALIVE

How should a Christian wife respond if her husband demands that she do something inappropriate, immoral, or destructive? (See: 1 Sam. 25:2–38, quiet, assertive wisdom; 1 Pet. 3:1, 2, respect with godly conduct.)

How does the authority of Scripture and conscience compare to the authority of a spouse or one's supervisor in the work place? (See: Ps. 1)

Explain how you might use the "law of relationship" (Matt. 22:37–40) to test behavior and determine appropriate response.

What two moral flaws dominate Ahasuerus's actions recorded in 1:10–13?

BIBLE EXTRA

What does Proverbs 31:3–5 say about drinking and the office of a king?

List the effects of excessive drinking noted in Proverbs 20:1; 23:29–33 and Isaiah 28:7.

How is anger related to power in Proverbs 16:32?

To what is anger compared in Proverbs 12:16; 14:17?

THE KING'S DECREES (1:13–22)

The king turns to his wise men to soothe his embarrassment and save his public image. Their advice is as foolish and unperceptive as his previous action.

WORD WEALTH

"Wise men who understood the times" (1:13) were the leading princes of Media and Persia skilled in matters of law and politics. Ahasuerus relied on them to advise him concerning politically sensitive issues (1 Chr. 12:32). Their response here shows the inferiority of wisdom which does not come from God (Jer. 10:7). They treat a problem in relationship as a matter of "law and justice."

What societal roles do the "wise men" assume will be greatly affected by Vashti's refusal? (v. 16)

What do the men fear women will do? Is this fear logical? (vv. 17, 18)

Does this same fear exist in modern society? How is this fear played out in the church today?

What two decrees were to be made? (vv. 19, 22)

What was the projected result of the decrees? (v. 20) In reality, what would be the most likely result of this legislation?

Is it possible to legislate respect or honor? According to Ephesians 5:22–33, what causes wives to truly respect and honor their husbands?

What does the king's quick acceptance of Memucan's suggestion tell you about him? (vv. 21, 22)

What two moral flaws dominate Ahasuerus' actions in 1:13–22?

The King's Remedy for Regret (2:1–4)

In hindsight, the king must have realized the foolishness of his impetuous action toward the queen. Persian law could not be reversed (1:19), and now the king feels the loss of Vashti. His servants who know him well soothe him with a new suggestion sure to appeal to Ahasuerus.

What was the attendants' plan (2:2–4)

Who was to gather the young women? From what geographical area were they to come? How many beautiful young virgins were to be rounded up? (2:2, 3)

Does the gathering of young virgins appear consensual on their part or mandatory? Do you suppose many women would have chosen this life? (2:3, 15)

What effect do you think this round-up had on the parents and young men of the provinces?

     WORD WEALTH

"Pleases" (2:4) literally means "shall be good in the eyes of."[10] The young woman who most appealed to the king's eyes would become queen instead of Vashti.

What two moral flaws dominate Ahasuerus's actions in 2:1–4?

Using your answers from each section of the text, list the prominent moral defects you noted in King Ahasuerus.
Esther 1:1–9

Esther 1:10–12

Esther 1:13–22

Esther 2:1–4

How does your list relate to 1 John 2:15–17?

What does that tell you about the foundation of Ahasuerus's wisdom? His motivation and use of opportunity?

Define your driving passions and purposes. What foundation do they imply?

FAITH ALIVE

The author's "sketch" of Ahasuerus provides a contrasting backdrop for the very different motivation and actions of Esther and Mordecai which will be seen in later chapters. Yet, like Joseph's Pharaoh, King Ahasuerus is used by God to promote and protect His people. Ahasuerus's blunder concerning Vashti is channeled by God to open an opportunity for His people.

Read 2 Chronicles 20:6 and Proverbs 21:1. What do these truths mean to you today?

How does understanding them change the way you think and live in the world?

Take time to praise God as King of the whole earth. Thank Him that He intervenes in the governments of the world. Thank Him that He sets the boundaries of the rule of wicked and just alike. Ask God to turn the hearts of our national and international leaders and raise Christians into high places in government.

1. "Opportunity," *Funk and Wagnalls Standard College Dictionary* (New York: Harcourt Brace, and World, Inc., 1966).

2. *Spirit-Filled Life Bible* (Nashville: Thomas Nelson, 1991), 669, "Chart: Ezra 8:36, The Times of Ezra, Nehemiah, and Esther."

3. F. B. Huey, Jr., *Esther*, The Expositor's Bible Commentary, vol. 4 (Grand Rapids: Zondervan Publishing House, 1988), 776–779, 784.

4. "Farce," *Webster's New Collegiate Dictionary, 8th edition* (Springfield: G & C Merriam Company, 1980).

5. *Spirit-Filled Life Bible*, 676, "Chart: Neh. 2:1, Persian Kings of the Restoration, 559–404 B.C."

6. "Ahasuerus," *Nelson's Illustrated Bible Dictionary* (Nashville: Thomas Nelson Publishers, 1986). Ibid., "Darius."

7. Joyce G. Baldwin, *Esther: An Introduction and Commentary*, Tyndale Old Testament Commentaries, ed. D. J. Wiseman (Downers Grove: Inter-Varsity, 1984), 18–19, 55–56. F. B. Huey, Jr., *Esther*, The Expositor's Bible Commentary, 779.

8. *Spirit-Filled Life Bible*, 697, note on Esther 1:3.

9. Ibid., 1195, "Word Wealth: Ezek. 28:12, beauty."

Lesson 8/Opportunity: Cooperating with God's Plan
(Esther 2:5–23)

A farmer living miles from town met with a serious accident which required that his wife drive him immediately to the hospital. As the wife half-pulled, half-carried her husband to the truck, she shouted instructions to her young son, telling him to latch the door and stay inside until the nearest neighbor arrived. The neighbor herself, however, was unavoidably delayed.

As dusk approached, the neighbor sped toward the little frame house. She could see the light of a lantern glowing softly through the front curtains and a little column of smoke rising from the chimney. Her frantic knock was answered by the lad's usual greeting. Amazed at his calm demeanor and the tidiness of the cottage, she asked the boy how he had managed.

The lad answered, "When it was past noon, I did not know what to do. Then I remembered that mother said I should always ask God to help me. So I kneeled beside the Bible stand where we always pray. It seemed clear: 'Do today as you always do.' So I gathered the eggs and filled the water bucket. When the little hand was on five, I had a slice of mother's bread, a piece of meat, a big glass of milk, and two cookies. Just before dark, I lighted the lantern and turned it low just like mother does. Then I added two logs to the fire just like father always does. And so I have continued until now."

In 2:5–23, Esther also suddenly finds herself in a totally unfamiliar environment in a situation which was not of her choosing. Instead of protesting or becoming bitter, Esther chooses to believe that God is in control and will help her. She cooperates with God's plan by continuing to do as she has always done. The humility, godly restraint, and respectful attitude which she has learned in Mordecai's house continues to be her pattern. And though her social position changes, Esther's relationship to Mordecai remains consistent even in his absence.

MORDECAI AND ESTHER: RELATIONSHIP (2:5–7)

As the first stage of God's plan to deliver His people unfolds, we are introduced to two of the main characters in the drama: Esther and Mordecai.

What information is given concerning Mordecai? (vv. 5, 6)

What additional information does 1 Samuel 9:1 and 2 offer concerning Mordecai's great-grandfather Kish?

BIBLE EXTRA

Read about the 597 B.C. captivity of Jerusalem by the Babylonians in which Kish was taken (2 Kin. 24:8–16). What status did Mordecai's ancestors likely hold in Jerusalem?

Mordecai was probably born in Babylonia during the years of the Jews' captivity. (The non-Hebrew name "Mordecai" is related to *Marduk,* the name of a Babylonian god.)[1] Like many of the Jews, his family decided to remain in Babylon after the Persian conquerors released the Jews to return to their homeland. How does Ezra 1:5 explain the fact that many did not return to Jerusalem?

Describe Esther's relationship to Mordecai (v. 7, 15).

WORD WEALTH

Esther (2:7), which means "star," is the Persian equivalent of Hebrew *Hadassah*, meaning "myrtle." The Persian name was probably given to Hadassah by Mordecai and used in their public life. The myrtle bears a flower which looks like a star. Myrtle branches, still used during the Feast of Tabernacles, represent peace and thanksgiving. The prophets Isaiah and Zechariah symbolize the Lord's forgiveness and acceptance of His people as the myrtle which replaces the thorns and briars of the desert (Is. 41:19; 55:13; Zech. 1:8).[2]

ESTHER'S PREPARATION (2:8–11)

Perhaps some young women of the Persian provinces found the idea of life in the palace and the possibility of becoming queen intriguing. Perhaps others from less prosperous families considered the rich provision of food and clothing and life in the harem a security to be desired. Yet one must wonder how many young women hid themselves and how many parents or lovers bribed the officers to overlook their daughters or fiancées. Surely many young women taken to the royal women's quarters had envisioned a very different life for themselves and now regretted their own beauty!

Esther, the Jewess, was herself one of the women taken to Shushan (v. 8). How do you suppose a Jew would think or feel about being selected for a Gentile king's harem?

Hegai, the virgins' custodian, was immediately pleased with Esther, that is, she "was good in his eyes" (v. 9). This first evaluation was based on appearance. Esther, being "beautiful in form and lovely to look at" (v. 7), was seen to be one of the most beautiful women of the provinces. Yet, Hegai's approval did not end there.

WORD WEALTH

"She obtained his favor" (2:9). This phrase implies more than the fact that Hegai would select Esther out of a lineup of beauty contestants. It may be translated literally: "she rose in favor before him."[3] As Hegai was around Esther, he increasingly appreciated her so that she obtained *hesed,* or his steadfast kindness and affectionate loyalty. Esther's attitude, personality, and conduct evidenced a humility and graciousness which supplemented her excellent outward appearance. Esther's inward and outward beauty won Hegai's heart!

FAITH ALIVE

Have you ever known a "beautiful" woman who became less and less attractive as you got to know her? Have you known a "plain" woman who became beautiful to you as her inward nature was revealed? In which of these categories would you fall?

Daniel, a captive in Babylon, obtained favor with his supervisor just as Esther did with Hegai. What was the secret of Daniel's favor? (Dan. 1:9)

What preceded that favor? (1:8) What followed his consistent dedication to God? (1:17–20; 2:48)

Certainly God has a purpose for every individual. What seems to be one "human factor" in successful availability for use in key roles in God's plan?

How are you evidencing your full availability for God's use of your particular life?

In what three ways did Hegai show that he favored Esther? (v. 9)

Verses 10 and 11 offer an inside look at the private life of Esther and Mordecai and their situation as Jews in a Gentile nation. What adjectives would you use to describe their relationship?

How did each maintain a strong relationship while physically separated? (vv. 10, 11) How might their activities parallel a close relationship with God?

According to Proverbs 13:1 and 3, in what two ways does Esther's behavior evidence wisdom and maturity? (v. 10)

Whether Mordecai and Esther generally followed the dietary codes and other stipulations of the Law is not known. While in Hegai's custody, it appears Esther freely received the king's food portions and other beauty preparations (v. 9). Given her Persian name and lack of usual Semitic restrictions, Esther's racial and religious identity would not be evident unless she revealed it.

 FAITH ALIVE

Anti-Semitism in Persia: Persians were generally tolerant of the religion and customs of the diverse people who made up the Persian Empire. Cyrus II (Dan. 5), who founded the Persian Empire, was humane and benevolent toward those he defeated. In the first year of his reign, Cyrus issued a decree restoring Jews to their homeland following the long captivity in Babylon (2 Chr. 36:22, 23; Ezra 1:1–4). Later, Darius (father of Ahasuerus) not only ordered work on the Jewish Temple at Jerusalem to resume after a fourteen-year stoppage, but gave a generous subsidy to finance the work (Ezra 6:1–12). And two of three returns to Jerusalem occurred during the reign of Artaxerxes I, Ahasuerus's successor (Ezra 7:1–28; Neh. 2:1–10; 13:6).

However, opposition from enemies surrounding Judah and Jerusalem occurred throughout the days of Cyrus and Darius, frustrating the attempts at rebuilding. During Ahasuerus's reign and the early years of Artaxerxes, the movement against the Jews in Judah reached all the way to Shushan. Letters were written against the Jews citing them as a rebellious people dangerous to the Empire (Ezra 4:4–7 ff).

Although Ahasuerus appeared uncommitted to choosing a new queen from the noble Persian families, an anti-Semitic current may have caused intolerance for a queen of known Jewish descent. Esther's disclosure of her race may have quelled Hegai's favor and doomed her to the life of a concubine.[4]

Ahasuerus's exorbitance and inflated sense of self-worth is seen in the extravagant preliminaries to a night with the king (vv. 12–14). Marriage preparations still followed by some in modern Iran and northern India may provide insight into the ancient procedures. Even today some brides-to-be participate in ritual cleansings and are treated for several months with beautifying body pastes which remove blemishes and lighten skin tone. Exfoliation of body hair, application of special masks for the face, hands, and feet, and the use of various facial make-ups are also included in this preparation.[5]

Surely during the year of perfumes and oils, much instruction also took place. Training in court decorum, conversation, the selection and wearing of clothing, and the artistic application of make-up would seem appropriate and necessary. Education as to the personal likes, dislikes, and idiosyncrasies of the king would most certainly be taught.

Each young woman's attitude and aptitude would become evident as her turn came to go in to the king. Her selection of clothing and jewelry would indicate her desire and goal. She could take what pleased her or what would please the king. The items she chose from the house of the women would go with her to the house of the concubines and become her "reward" if she was not selected queen (vv. 13, 14).

FAITH ALIVE

In a similar way, our hearts are tested when we enter the presence of our King. When you go in before Him, is your goal what you may obtain? Or is your heart's desire relationship? Does your daily life reflect times of intense preparation—study, prayer, worship and meditation upon Him—which will make you pleasing to the King? Does the fragrance of His presence and the anointing of His Spirit mark your life?

Take time to surrender your heart-goals to God. Ask Him to begin an intensive season of purification and consecration in your life. Ask God to renew the fear (reverent respect) of Him in your life. Tell Him that you want to become a delight to Him. Commit yourself to the disciplines which beautify your conversation, personality, and ways. As you pray, write down the specific things the Lord lays on your heart.

ESTHER'S PRESENTATION (2:15–18)

The pagan king Ahasuerus most certainly did not understand the difference between Esther and the other women or the significance of the timing of her presentation. Yet surely God arranged the day Esther was to go in to the king as He also ordered the other events which make up her story.

WORD WEALTH

Tebeth was the tenth month of the Babylonian calendar. This mid-winter month (December/January) was a cold and rainy season in Shushan. The seventh year of Ahasuerus's reign was four years after Vashti ("the desired one," "the best," or "the beloved") was banished.[6]

What a great contrast Esther's beauty must have been to the grayness of the Persian winter! Adorned by God's anointing, Esther obtained favor with Hegai and all who saw her. Esther never had to go to the house of the concubines, for Ahasuerus made up his mind immediately.

What does Esther's selection from the house of women tell you about her attitude and goal when presenting herself to the king? (v. 15)

The king's "love" for Esther could be anything from carnal attraction to true affection. Whatever the case, Esther found favor (*hesed*) with Ahasuerus as with Hegai so that kindness and loyalty marked his relationship to her, and he crowned her queen (v. 17). As Esther—"Star"—delighted the king so the drab winter was brightened for the king's officials and servants by a feast in her honor. Ahasuerus's joy was generously extended to the provinces. The "holiday" and the giving of "gifts" likely included a day's rest from labor, some form of tax relief, and special presents of food (v. 18).[7]

ESTHER AND MORDECAI: TEAMWORK (2:19–23)

Many important threads of the unfolding plot of the Book of Esther are exposed in this last section of chapter 2. The first two verses are probably a recap of 2:8 and 10. "A second time" (v. 19) may bear the sense of restating the chapter 2 events prior to Esther's coronation.[8]

During the year of Esther's preparation, Mordecai occupied a position of honor which gave him some access to the king's court (v. 19). His sitting at the king's gate likely involved service in some legal capacity (v. 19; see Dan. 2:48, 49). How might Mordecai's position give an even greater reason for Esther not to disclose her family ties? (vv. 19, 20)

The plot uncovered by Mordecai (v. 21) was not uncommon in palace politics. Ahasuerus was murdered fourteen years later (464 B.C.) by a courtier.[9] Here, Mordecai prevents Bigthan (see 1:10; 6:2) and Teresh from "laying hands on" or assassinating the king. Esther, having greater access to the king, channels the information to Ahasuerus in Mordecai's name with the result that the culprits are hanged. The fact that Mordecai was not rewarded in some way when this event was recorded in the chronicles of the Persian kings is so unusual that the oversight must be attributed to providential intervention by God.

 PROBING THE DEPTHS

The way in which Esther and Mordecai work as a team behind the scene may have significance beyond the literal facts. Perhaps some symbolism is intended to illustrate the "active hiddenness" of the unnamed, anonymous God of the Book of Esther. Perhaps Esther signifies the discrete, yielded servant who can be mightily used of God, and Mordecai signifies the secret but constant providential care of God as He warns, prepares, and unravels. Their lives are "hidden" in the very center of public life and government in a Gentile nation just as the Hand of the Sovereign God who "rules over all the kingdoms of the nations" often appears invisible and unnoticed (2 Chr. 20:6).

 FAITH ALIVE

Read the following references and notice how God put key factors in place which will bring deliverance for His people even before their need for deliverance is known.

Uncovering of the assassination plot	2:21–23	----------------➤ 6:1–3
Esther's hidden identity	2:10, 20	----------------➤ 7:4
Esther's position and favor	2:17	----------------➤ 7:2; 8:1, 4–6

Read Isaiah 46:10 and Romans 8:28. What do these verses and the illustration presented above tell you about God's activity in your life?

What difference does that make to you today? In the future?

1. "Mordecai," *Nelson's Illustrated Bible Dictionary* (Nashville: Thomas Nelson Publishers, 1986).

2. Joyce G. Baldwin, *Esther: An Introduction and Commentary,* Tyndale Old Testament Commentaries, ed. D. J. Wiseman (Downers Grove: InterVarsity Press, 1984), 65–66.

3. Jay P. Green, Sr., ed. and trans., *The Interlinear Hebrew-Aramaic Old Testament* (Peabody: Hendrickson, 1985), II:1304.

4. "Persia," *Nelson's Illustrated Bible Dictionary.*

5. Joyce G. Baldwin, *Esther: An Introduction and Commentary,* 68.

6. Ibid., 69.

7. R. Laird Harris, Gleason L. Archer, Jr., and Bruce K. Waltke, eds., *Theological Wordbook of the Old Testament* (Chicago: Moody Press, 1980), nos. 1323d, 1421h.

8. *Spirit-Filled Life Bible* (Nashville: Thomas Nelson Publishers, 1991), 699, note on Esther 2:19.

9. "Ahasuerus," *Nelson's Illustrated Bible Dictionary.*

Lesson 9/Opportunity: Announcing Allegiance
(Esther 3:1—4:3)

A simple experiment is commonly conducted in elementary school science to demonstrate the concept of surface tension. A glass bowl is partially filled with water, and visible particles such as pencil shavings or coffee grounds are sprinkled on the surface of the water. The particles randomly and uniformly cover the water's surface. When a tablespoon of powdered laundry detergent is sprinkled in the middle of the water, the surface tension instantly changes. The floating particles rush to the sides of the bowl and clump together in tight groups making them easily distinguishable.

Something very similar to this reaction takes place in the third chapter of Esther. Mordecai takes a stand for the God of Israel and the people at the gate quickly polarize. Haman emerges as a clearly distinguishable and formidable enemy and draws others around him in a vendetta against the Jews.

MORDECAI'S STAND (3:1–6)

The introduction of Haman concludes the cast of main characters and sets in motion the central plot of the Book of Esther. During the four-year span between Esther's coronation (2:16, 17) and the act recorded in 3:7, Haman rose to power above all the princes of Persia and Media who advised the king. Since Haman is not listed among the seven princes during Ahasuerus's third year (1:14), he must have ascended to prime minister very quickly.

What facts are given concerning Haman? (3:1, 2)

BIBLE EXTRA

No information is available about Hammedatha, but the Agagites were infamous in Israel's history. The name derives from King Agag, the leader of the Amalekites. The Amalekites—a term virtually synonymous with "enemy of the Jews"—attacked Israel in the wilderness near Sinai. Read the word of the Lord to Moses which is recorded in Exodus 17:14–16 concerning this enemy.

Scan 1 Samuel 15:10–33 and 2 Samuel 1:12–14, which explain King Saul's loss of both his throne and life because of his failure to deal properly with the Agagites.

Could Mordecai as a descendant of Saul and Haman as a descendant of Agag be archetypes of a renewed battle against the archenemy of God's people? How could the outcome of this encounter foretell things to come? How does it speak to us today?

What was the royal command concerning Haman? What may have provoked such a decree? (v. 2)

How did Mordecai respond to this requirement? What was his reasoning? (vv. 2–4)

BEHIND THE SCENES

Most people think of Shadrach, Meshach, and Abed-Nego when a refusal to bow is mentioned. The three Hebrews, however, were asked to bow to an image of gold (Dan. 3:12). It was quite common for Jews and other peoples of the East to bow to those in high office or those whom they respected. When Abraham bowed to the sons of Heth—Canaanites (Gen. 23:7), Jacob bowed to Esau (Gen. 33:3), and Jacob's sons bowed to Joseph—the governor of Egypt (Gen. 42:6), they did not violate the second commandment (Ex. 20:4–6).

The simple honoring of an office would present no problems for a cosmopolitan Jew who taught his daughter humility and respect and allowed her to marry a Gentile king. Two issues seem to be involved here: (1) an inordinate show of undue honor and (2) the fact that Mordecai was a Jew and Haman was an Agagite. Mordecai would not bow to the archenemy of his people and a man who deserved no respect.

How can you tell that until this time, Mordecai had lived his public life as a Persian? (v. 4)

What does the way in which Mordecai's colleagues deal with him tell you about Mordecai the worker and man? (vv. 3, 4)

Mordecai's experience shows what Christians may expect when taking a stand in the secular world. What principles concerning tolerance of Christian values in the workplace may be gleaned from Haman's wrath and the colleagues final actions?

What great character defect is behind Haman's overflowing wrath? (v. 5; see Dan. 3:13, 19; 4:25). What form did Haman's wrath take? (v. 6)

 FAITH ALIVE

Haman could have had Mordecai arrested and hanged as an example and warning to all the Jews and other residents of Shushan, but this act would not quell his intense hatred. The deep wickedness of Haman's heart is revealed by his desire to destroy all of Mordecai's people not only in

Shushan but throughout the entire Persian Empire. When we read Haman's heart-thoughts, we want to hiss at his name as is the Jewish custom when a terrible villain is mentioned.

But before we hiss at Haman's name, we must determine if any racial hatred resides in us. It is unlikely that one growing up in the USA could escape harboring some racial prejudice and enmity—either consciously or unconsciously. The Sunday "church hour" in America is still the most segregated hour of the week.

When we cannot see all people groups as those made in God's image, we are guilty of the heinous sin of racial hatred. When we lump a person into a category based on the past acts of others, stereotypes, and carnal systems of power and place, the sin of racial hatred dwells in us. This sinful way of thinking and being denies the wisdom of the Creator God, scoffs at the love of the Father and the grace of Christ, and resists the Spirit of God who indwells, gifts, and appoints people of all nations and races.

Ask God to uncover racial hatred and prejudice in your heart and life. Ask Him to open the Word to you concerning this issue. Confess your sins. Act upon that confession and your renewed mind. Ask God to work the discipline of unity and love into your life and that of your local church (Eph. 4; 1 Cor. 13). Then, be ready to let God use you to bring healing and reconciliation.

HAMAN'S SCHEME (3:7–11)

Haman clearly reveals his reprehensible nature and craftiness as he plots the destruction of the Jews. His own disrespect for authority is revealed by his deceitful manipulation of the king.

Haman precedes his audience with the king by seeking an omen which will indicate the most favorable day to execute his vengeance. He casts the *Pur.*

     WORD WEALTH

Pur, or lot, is a cube-shaped dice used in the ancient East to determine many things. Its use illustrates the common Eastern belief in a predetermined fate with which one must cooperate to be successful. During the reign of the Assyrian king Shalmaneser III (858 to 824 B.C.), a whole year's events were determined on New Year's Day by the casting of the lot. The *pur* becomes very important to the message and purpose of the Book of Esther.[1]

Contrary to the fatalistic Eastern view, Jewish faith and Scripture show the providence of the uncontrollable God. Read the references and list two ways God's providence is manifested.

1. Proverbs 16:33:

2. Esther 9:24–26:

List the three deceitful manipulations Haman uses to draw Ahasuerus into his plan (vv. 8, 9)

(1) Exaggerations which distort the truth:

(2) A bold-faced lie:

(3) A bribe:

What title does the author award Haman for his success in manipulating the king? (v. 10) Read Proverbs 6:16–19 and list the ways Haman has also shown himself an enemy of God.

What is the king's immediate response to Haman's request? (v. 10)

BEHIND THE SCENES

A king's **signet ring** was an emblem of royal authority. Such a ring had raised features which could be pressed into wax or clay to leave an imprint—usually a name or an identifying symbol. Signet rings were widely used in ancient times and functioned much as personal signatures do today.[2]

It is impossible to tell if Ahasuerus agrees with Haman because he trusts Haman, he lives in fear of revolt, he is motivated by greed, or all three. When Ahasuerus gives his stamp of approval, he does not even know the name of the people he is allowing to be exterminated! Not only has Ahasuerus not learned from his action against Vashti, but he shows himself to be a fool.

Read Esther 1:9; 2:15, and Proverbs 18:13. Then explain how the king's foolishness is compounded.

Ahasuerus's statement in verse 11 was most likely not a refusal of the large sum Haman offered him (see 4:7). He was saying that wealthy Haman could use his own money as he liked.[3] In the same way, the unnamed people were now Haman's, and he was free to dispose of them as well (v. 11).

THE KING'S DECREE (3:12–15)

Haman spares no time in calling the scribes to take his dictation. The hundreds of documents are written forthwith in Haman's own words and according to all that was in his heart. Decrees were to be delivered to satraps—rulers of the Persian provinces—governors, who assisted the satraps, and local leaders—chieftains of the tribal groups (v. 12).[4]

The haste of the couriers rushing to every city and rural community parallels the king's hasty decision and again draws attention to his foolishness. The foolhardy nature of the act is also made plain by the wisdom of Proverbs 29:2 and the reaction of the people in the Citadel (v. 15). How does the confusion and perplexity at Shushan both confirm that Haman acted deceitfully

(vv. 8, 9) and function to undermine rather than strengthen loyalty to the king?

Read John 10:10 and note the parallels in Esther 3:13. What do these facts say about Haman's inspiration?

PROBING THE DEPTHS

Spirit of the Antichrist? The slaughter of women who would have no means of defense and children who couldn't possibly be guilty of rebellion against the king shows the depths of Haman's ruthlessness and pride. It becomes clear that Haman's desire was not that men bow in respect for his office and authority, but that they bow and pay homage to Haman as deity (3:5). He takes upon himself the power of life, death, and judgment in a great ethnic purge. Like the Roman emperors Gaius Caligula and Domitian (A.D. 37–41, 81–96) and Hitler of Nazi Germany, Haman demonstrates the corrupting potential of political power which will mark the final Man of Sin.

As Haman stands against all who represent the true God, the final Man of Sin, the Antichrist, will stand in opposition to all that Jesus Christ represents. Speaking arrogant and boastful words, the Final Antichrist, who receives his authority and power from Satan, will make the entire world worship him.

Just as the aging apostle John noted the presence of the spirit of Antichrist in the world in his day, so that same spirit now exists. It motivates the present-day ethnic purges in Bosnia and elsewhere and the martyrdoms of the saints around the world. In a lesser way, agreement with that same spirit is at the root of every racial hatred and prejudice and every arrogance and pride which intentionally defames another's godly character (See: Dan. 7:25; 8:25; 11:36; John 17:12; 2 Thess. 2:3, 4; 1 Tim. 4:1; 1 John 2:18, 22; 4:3; 2 John 7; Rev. 13:11, 12).[5]

THE JEWS' LAMENT (4:1–3)

As morning folded into afternoon, Ahasuerus and Haman "sat down to drink" (3:15). The citizens of Shushan expressed their puzzlement to one another in the marketplace and home. But the Jews throughout the provinces began to wail. And many lay in sackcloth and ashes refusing the evening meal.

BEHIND THE SCENES

Mourning was and is more freely expressed in the East than in the West. Loud wailing and crying accompanied the death of a loved one (Mark 5:38). The donning of sackcloth and the wearing of ashes symbolized great grief, self-abasement, and contrition. The mourner's clothes were often torn and a rough strip of dark "sackcloth"—usually goat's hair—was draped across the bare chest. When worn by priests, those in authority, or the people as a whole, the stark contrast of this clothing to the usual apparel symbolized a corporate calamity. The sight itself was a call to repentance, prayer, and fasting and a plea to God for His intervention (Joel 1:13–15; 2:12–19; Jon. 3:5).

One entering the king's gate in sackcloth might be slain on sight, especially if the king were nearby. What two reasons would Mordecai have for getting as close to the gate as possible? (v. 2)

FAITH ALIVE

The events of Esther 3:3—4:3 were all brought about by Mordecai's refusal to bow to Haman. In light of the results of Mordecai's action, do you think his refusal was right? Justified? Wise? Why?

Read Romans 13:1–7 which discusses the Christian's civil responsibilities. In light of this passage, study the examples of at least two of the following people who disobeyed civil authority: Daniel and the three Hebrews (Dan. 1, 3), the Hebrew midwives (Ex. 1:15–22), the apostles (Acts 5:27–33). List the principles gleaned from these stories which could assist you in determining the correct action to take in a situation where faith and law are in conflict.

A Christian's action is often seen by the unsaved as characteristic of Christians in general. But a Christian leader's actions are always viewed as representative and symbolic of the group of people he or she leads. Thus, the action of one person may have widespread influence to help or harm the entire group and the cause of Christ. Read James 3:1, 2, 13, 17, 18. List the "tests" which show if leaders (or mature Christians) truly exemplify Jesus.

Is your life helping or hurting the cause of Christ? How? What will you do about it?

Are you beginning to exhibit the characteristics of one who will be a wise leader? In what ways? What areas do you need to submit to God?

Ask God to help you begin to be transformed in one of these areas. Make study of Scripture passages which deal specifically with this area part of your daily devotions. Ask God to give you opportunities to practice this Christian grace. Jot down encouraging progress notes as you begin to see victory in this area.

1. Joyce G. Baldwin, *Esther: An Introduction and Commentary,* Tyndale Old Testament Commentaries, ed. D. J. Wiseman (Downers Grove: InterVarsity Press, 1984), 22–23.

2. "Seal," *Nelson's Illustrated Bible Dictionary* (Nashville: Thomas Nelson Publishers, 1986). "Signet," *Nelson's Illustrated Bible Dictionary.*

3. Joyce G. Baldwin, *Esther: An Introduction and Commentary,* 74.

4. *Spirit-Filled Life Bible* (Nashville: Thomas Nelson Publishers, 1991), 700, note on Esther 3:12.

5. Ibid., 1836, note on 2 Thessalonians 2:4. "Antichrist, The," *Nelson's Illustrated Bible Dictionary.*

Lesson 10/Opportunity: Identifying with the Distressed
(Esther 4:4–17)

Turning point: a divinely engineered moment when life's focus shifts from self or trivia, and mind, emotion, and spirit are suddenly fastened to purpose in an indissoluble union; a cross-over in spiritual life and meaning which brings full answer to one's life-mission.

Such "moments" seem not to be sought and found, but rather to capture those whose hearts are yielded to God as they faithfully do what they know to do. Such a moment "happened" to one holy Sister on the edge of a filthy street corner in a foreign city. As she became one with the pain and brokenness of the dying man she cradled in her lap, an international ministry to the poor, oppressed, and infirm was spawned. For Tom it happened the first time he saw a woman beaten almost beyond recognition by the man who vowed to love and cherish her. A counseling center and shelter for battered women was conceived in that moment. The "cross-over" came for Jane during an intense moment of prayer when her heart-cry for another touched the very heart compassion of God, and a true ministry of intercession was born.

Such a turning point also takes place in the account recorded in Esther 4:4–17. Esther is transformed, never to be the same again. When the Jews' desperate need pierces her heart, she picks up faith and marches forward grasping opportunity. A mature passion for mission is born which enables her to willingly risk her life for the sake of her people. Esther, the young woman of grace and beauty, becomes Queen Esther the Jewess, a woman of great courage, authority, and purpose.

THE UNVEILING OF PERIL (4:4–9)

In this first section of the text any sense of disconnection Esther may have felt between herself and her people is dissolved. As Esther freely opens her heart to feel the unnamed distress Mordecai the Jew suffers, she is suddenly hooked to the plight of her people.

The ongoing bond between Mordecai and Esther was well known to Esther's maids and eunuchs who had long been her messengers (v. 4). When Mordecai, the respectable Persian official of the king, appeared outside the gate dressed in sackcloth and howling with grief, Esther's little entourage hastened to their queen. As soon as Esther heard their report, she became "deeply distressed."

WORD WEALTH

"Deeply distressed" (4:4), as used here means writhed in great emotional anguish and pain. The verb, which may be translated "travail, be in anguish, be pained, dance, whirl, writhe, fear, tremble," contains the idea of motion—either a whirling motion or a writhing in labor pains. It may also encompass the emotions and attitudes related to these movements. The same intensive form used in Esther 4:4 elsewhere describes the pain of a wicked man (Job 15:20) and a great whirlwind (Jer. 23:19).[1]

Have you ever been far away when someone you loved was in great anguish? Like Esther, we would want to "take their sackcloth away from them." Why do you think Esther was shocked? What do you think she thought had happened? Why do you suppose Mordecai refused the garments? (v. 4)

Although Esther was not far away in terms of distance, she was confined to the women's quarters and gardens and was unable to casually walk about the court or the city. Esther's confidence in Hathach's loyalty is indicated by the fact that she did not send the maids or eunuchs who first brought the report. She specifically calls Hathach to secure all the details of Mordecai's distress. In great contrast to Mordecai's former discretion and secrecy, this conversation takes place in the market square (vv. 5, 6).

What three things does Mordecai share? What is the purpose behind his disclosures? (vv. 7, 8)

1.

2.

3.

Mordecai's position at the gate gave him access to information others may not have known. All of the king's loyal servants probably heard the decree at its first public reading, and a copy may have been easy enough to obtain. Which of the disclosures you listed above seems "odd"? Why do you think Mordecai emphasizes this particular fact? What part may it play in the battle Esther will soon face?

Mordecai does not simply suggest or urge Esther to petition the king on the Jews' behalf. As a father to his daughter, Mordecai tells Esther what to do. He commands her to use her influence to persuade the king to stop the upcoming atrocities. Mordecai's foresight in sending a copy of the decree assures that Esther will be convinced of the validity of the second-hand report she receives from Hathach (vv. 8, 9).

THE ASSESSMENT OF COST (4:10–12)

The communication between Esther and Mordecai becomes even more important at this point. Exact words are recorded verbatim. Perhaps Esther was voicing her fear and unwillingness to take a full stand on behalf of her people. But it seems more likely that she is asking Mordecai for help. To offer wise guidance he must have an accurate assessment of her situation. Esther reminds Mordecai of the law, and she adds personal information. In a sense she says: "You understand the risk of this procedure and my situation, don't you?" Esther may not know about the business of the kingdom, but after five years as queen, she did know Ahasuerus's foibles and fickleness!

     KINGDOM EXTRA

The Elements of Esther's Statement (v. 11)	
1	The Law of Access is universal for those of official status and the common people.
2	To enter the king's inner court without prior invitation means sure death for anyone.
3	The only exception to instant death is the king's special mercy and favor.
4	My favor with the king has greatly waned.

Assessment of the Present Situation: Although I am queen, I may have no influence unless Ahasuerus's heart is changed toward me and his favor is renewed.

     BEHIND THE SCENES

It likely was not much easier to gain audience with the King of Persia than it is to see a top U.S. government executive today. The seven princes seem to have had considerable access to the king's presence (1:14; 6:4). Officials like Mordecai had access to the king's gate, a few top officials might come into the outer courts, but only a small handful of trusted servants traversed the inner court to the throne room or the private apartments of the king (6:2, 4). All others must be called by the king. Intruders would be slain as they approached unless the king quickly held out his scepter—the official staff symbolizing his power and authority (4:11).[2] If the scepter was extended, the suppliant would live.

 WORD WEALTH

Live, *chayah,* means to live, to stay alive, be preserved; to flourish, to enjoy life; to live in happiness; be alive, recover health, live continuously.[3]

Read Esther 2:14 and 4:11. Why could Esther presume no special favor with the king?

 FAITH ALIVE

Using the items in "The Elements of Esther's Statement (v. 11)", contrast the superficial and wavering acceptance of King Ahasuerus with the wonderful acceptance of the King of kings. Read the references below. Then write your own final conclusion based on those verses.

Access to the King of Kings		
1	Full universal opportunity:	John 3:15–17; Matt. 11:28–30
	Full invitation:	Matt. 7:7, 8; Rev. 22:17
3	Full life:	Ps. 16:5, 6, 11; John 10:9, 10
	Full unwavering favor:	John 6:37–40; Rom. 8:32
My Conclusions Based on the Above:		

THE BIRTH OF AN INTERCESSOR (4:13–17)

This section of text is the most powerful and the most often quoted in the Book of Esther. The event recorded here forms the watershed moment in the account of the Jews' deliverance; all events lead up to this moment and all following events are a result of this decisive moment. Mordecai and Esther's words are again recorded as exact speech.

It seems that Mordecai understood Esther's previous message as a refusal. He, too, gives an assessment of the situation. His strong words of exhortation and caution become for Esther words of empowerment which challenge her to fulfill her destiny.

What two results does Mordecai declare Esther will experience if she does not speak for the Jews? (v. 14)

1.

2.

What do these statements show about Mordecai's concept of providence (God's sovereign control) and an individual's call to ministry? (v. 14)

    WORD WEALTH

The Hebrew words which lie behind "relief" and "deliverance" (4:14) come from interesting root words. **Relief** derives from a word meaning "be wide, spacious." Elsewhere, it is translated "space, interval" (see Gen. 32:17).[4] The "relief" which is to be experienced is literally a "wide place." The Jews, who are now hemmed in on all sides and unable to move in their own defense, will be given temporary respite from this constraint. **Deliverance** will be rescue from their present situation.

Rewrite Mordecai's powerful conclusion in your own words. (v. 14b)

What effect do Mordecai's words have on Esther? Describe the abrupt and dramatic change which takes place in her. (vv. 15, 16)

Esther's famous words of verse 16 read: "If I perish, I perish." How do these words parallel Jesus' words in John 12:23–26?

Is it possible for anyone to serve the cause of Christ without dying? What are some "deaths" a person must experience in order to effectively serve in any ministry?

As Esther moves from her state of passive dependency on Mordecai to a stance of authority and action, is she more or less "dependent"? How? (vv. 16, 17)

What is Mordecai's response to Esther's newfound strength? (vv. 16, 17)

AT A GLANCE

Esther's commandment to Mordecai is both an acceptance of her destiny and a confession of faith that God can and will use her. Although the deliverance Esther brought was only temporary, it foreshadowed the great rescue which would appear in a future age. In accepting her destiny, Esther became a picture of Jesus Christ, in His roles of Servant, Priest, and Savior.

Esther: Revealing Christ to the Nation	
Role	How Revealed by Esther
Servant	Lived in submission, humility, dependence, and obedience; maintained unity with Mordecai (Esth. 2; 4; 9:29–32; John 4:34; 6:38)
Priest	Fully identified herself with the distressed; interceded before God and the king on their behalf (Esth. 4:16; Heb. 2:17; Matt. 4:2; John 17:20)
Savior	Gave up her right to live in order to save the nation from certain death; was exalted by the king (Esth. 4–9; Mark 10:45; 1 Tim. 2:5, 6; Phil. 2:5–11)[5]

Describe the fast Esther orders in terms of who is to fast, when, why, and how. (v. 16)

BIBLE EXTRA

Fasting: Esther's directive to fast certainly required abstinence from food, but at its heart was a request for powerful prayer. Isaiah had cautioned that fasting as ritual had no significance (Is. 58). Yet when true fasting as a natural and appropriate result of deep emotional concern is accompanied by prayer, it demonstrates the sincerity and intense desire of the petitioner. Israel's history was filled with accounts of the powerful effects of such heartfelt prayer. (See: Deut. 9:9, 25; Ezra. 8:21–23; Is. 36:1—37:38; Joel 2:12–18; Jon. 3:5–10).

Sustained prayer with a particular focus brought powerful deliverance in the early church (Acts 12:1–17). And fasting and prayer gave birth to new and empowered ministry (Acts 13:1—14:28). As the one who would stand in the gap and perform the visible role in deliverance, Esther and her mission were to be the focus of petitions.

According to Old and New Testament Scripture, why is it important that we engage in spiritual warfare before any and all ministry takes place? (See: Zech. 4:6; Matt. 12:29; Eph. 6:12.)

BIBLE EXTRA

Spiritual Warfare: One of the church's greatest demands is to discern between spiritual struggle and social, personal, and political difficulty. Otherwise, believers may become detoured, wrestling with human adversaries instead of prayerfully warring against the invisible works of hell. In Ephesians 6:10–18, the apostle Paul warns of a clearly defined structure in the invisible realm. He describes the offensive weapons to be used in prayer. To put on the spiritual armor of God described in Ephesians 6 is to prepare for the battle. But prayer is the battle itself with God's word as the chief weapon. (See Eph. 6:10–18 for further study).[6]

PROBING THE DEPTHS

The Book of Esther challenges every individual and group of believers to recognize God's willingness and desire to use in a powerful way anyone who will surrender his or her will to His plan. Yet, it also shows the important part others play in the acceptance and performance of that very mission.

Like Esther, many women in the body of Christ have difficulty hearing and answering their call to destiny. Too often, Christians who are female are either subtly or clearly cautioned by their local church environment to be silent, passive, and to maintain the cultural "feminine ideal." Certainly many women never make the transition to move in full confidence and authority in their ministry call, especially when that ministry is nontraditional and highly visible.

Esther's transformation helps show how individuals and the church may assist women in fulfilling their God-given destiny:

- Her destiny, or ministry potential, was recognized and spoken aloud by a respected authority figure.
- Esther was fortified by the intercession and support of her community as she prepared herself to step out in faith. In fact, it is questionable as to whether her mission could have been successful without this mutual "owning" of her ministry and mission.
- She was facilitated by a mentor who: (1) recognized that the anointing and authority upon her was from God, (2) willingly yielded to that authority, and (3) worked with her as a team player toward a common spiritual purpose.

 ## FAITH ALIVE

Several stages may be noted in the process Esther went through to become actively engaged in her ministry call.

STAGES IN MINISTRY	GOAL OF THAT STAGE
1. Felt, saw, heard the desperate need of the Jews ---------➤	Understanding of the need and deep, emotional desire to help bear suffering and resolve crises
2. Clearly understood the high cost -------➤ of responding to that need	Fully informed answer led to an unwavering commitment
3. Firm decision -------➤	Preparation (both personal and assisted by others)
4. Spiritual preparation ---------➤	Authoritative action which exhibits wisdom and sensitivity to the Holy Spirit's guidance

Which stage of ministry best describes you now?

People who become discouraged or never follow through on their ministry call usually do so because they did not fully reach the goals of stage 2 or 3—they have not understood or paid the cost or they are not fully prepared for that ministry. This breakdown could be caused by a personal lack of spiritual commitment and devotion to God or lack of information or mentoring. If either of these describes you, stop now and recommit yourself to God. Ask Him to direct you to someone in your area of ministry call who will mentor you. Be willing to fully submit yourself to their instruction.

1. R. Laird Harris, Gleason L. Archer, Jr., and Bruce K. Waltke, eds., *Theological Wordbook of the Old Testament* (Chicago: Moody Press, 1980), 270–271, no. 623.

2. "Scepter," *Nelson's Illustrated Bible Dictionary* (Nashville: Thomas Nelson Publishers, 1986).

3. *Spirit-Filled Life Bible* (Nashville: Thomas Nelson Publishers, 1991), 1342, "Word Wealth: Hab. 2:4, shall live *chayah*."

4. R. Laird Harris, Gleason L. Archer, Jr., and Bruce K. Waltke, eds., *Theological Wordbook of the Old Testament*, 594, 837, nos. 1404a, 2132a.

5. *Spirit-Filled Life Bible*, 696, "Esther: Introduction, Christ Revealed."

6. Ibid., 1796, note on Eph. 6:12. Ibid., 1797, "Kingdom Dynamics: Eph. 6:10–18, Spiritual Warfare."

Lesson 11/Opportunity: Moving with the Spirit *(Esther 5:1—6:14)*

"The battle is not yours, but God's . . . Position yourselves, stand still and see the salvation of the Lord, who is with you . . . tomorrow go out . . ." (2 Chr. 20:15–17). These encouraging prophetic words concerning the enemies of Judah were delivered to King Jehoshaphat and his people following sincere fasting and prayer. Yet, they could just as well have been spoken to Esther and the Jews. As God "set ambushes against" Jehoshaphat's enemies so that they slew one another, God arranges Haman's demise as Esther and Mordecai stand in their positions and watch the Lord act. Just as God set the timing of Jehoshaphat's "battle," so He directs Esther who wisely waits another day for the right moment to present her petition.

The events of Esther 5 and 6 are full of great contrasts as God acts behind the scenes on the Jews' behalf. Ahasuerus extends his favor to Esther (5:1–5), yet she withholds her petition from him (5:6–8). Haman plans Mordecai's demise (5:9–14), yet Mordecai's rise is proclaimed (6:1–11) and Haman's doom is foretold (6:12–14).

ESTHER BIDES HER TIME (5:1–8)

The faith Esther demonstrated in 4:16 has not waned. After three days of united fasting and spiritual warfare, Esther acts with added confidence and keen wisdom. In concert with the Spirit's leading, Esther boldly initiates, yet also wisely delays.

How does Esther dress to appear before the king? What advantage might this dress bring? (5:1)

In what two ways does the king respond when he sees Esther? (5:2, 3)

WORD WEALTH

The prayers of the people which have been focused on Esther are being answered: "she found favor in his sight." **Favor** (5:2), *chen,* means grace, kindness, beauty, charm, pleasantness, or affectionate regard. The root *chanan* means "to act graciously or mercifully toward someone; to be compassionate, to be favorably inclined." Thus, it places emphasis on the recipient. As Esther stood at the edge of the inner court, she literally "rose in grace" in Ahasuerus's eyes.[1]

FAITH ALIVE

Esther showed that confidence and humility need not be opposing characteristics. Like Esther, we should come boldly before our King rightly clothed and with a right attitude. Below are some of the "royal robes" which remind God of our relationship and activate His compassion toward us. What else might be added to this list?

- A humble and contrite spirit   Is. 57:15
- Spirit of adoption crying "Abba"   Rom. 8:15
- Seal of the righteousness of faith   Rom. 4:11
- Jesus' name   John 16:23, 24

• Spiritual cleanness	Zech. 3:4; Rev. 3:5, 18
• Our legitimate needs	Heb. 4:15, 16
•	
•	
•	

BEHIND THE SCENES

Court Protocol: Esther's bold actions are tempered by her strict adherence to her training. Court protocol required that the king's graciousness be acknowledged. Touching the top of the royal scepter (and likely bowing or prostrating one-self) showed that one came under the king's authority. To not do so at this point would have been an insult which might have angered the king.

WORD WEALTH

"Up to half the kingdom" was a conventional term something like: "If you asked for the moon, I would give it to you." The king does not mean for Esther to lightly presume upon his goodness. Yet, at the same time, this phrase indicates Ahasuerus's eagerness to say "yes" to her petition (5:3, 6).[2]

In what ways is Esther's request surprising? Diplomatic? Discerningly wise? Appealing to the "male ego"? Effective? Faith-filled? (vv. 4, 5)

To invite Haman, the enemy of the Jews, to the banquet may appear dangerous or even foolish on Esther's part. How is it evident that this wisdom was from God? (v. 4, 5; see 5:9a, 12)

BEHIND THE SCENES

> The king poses his second question during the **"ban-quet of wine"** (v. 6). Leisurely Eastern banquets, or feasts, were usually concluded with a course of wines. At such a time, guests were full, amiable, and relaxed as they reclined on their couches and sipped after-dinner wine (1:6). Important matters were often discussed at this time. In such an atmosphere, one might feel free to make a request which would have been difficult earlier.[3]

How does Esther answer the king's second inquiry? What risks might be involved in this further delay? (vv. 7, 8)

Esther evidently did not sense a "go ahead" concerning voicing her petition and perceived that making her request now would be forcing the issue. Later there are clear signs that God has turned the situation, and it is time to make her move (6:11).

God does not always give a prophetic sign signaling correct timing. But when one is moving according to biblical principles and is called to a certain task or ministry, God will give assurance by his Spirit. This assurance may be a deep peace concerning the action and an inner unity of mind, emotions, and Spirit. Such a decision will "seem good to the Holy Spirit" and to you (Acts 15:28).

HAMAN PLANS MORDECAI'S DEMISE (5:9–14)

Haman's behavior recorded in 5:9–14 stands in stark contrast to Esther's behavior recorded in 5:1–8. Esther exhibited godly wisdom and humility which caused her to be in full control of the proceedings of the banquet. Haman exhibits a foolish pride which totally controls him.

Haman leaves Esther's banquet in high spirits, but the effects of the banquet upon Haman run much deeper than a festive attitude. Heady with a sense of his own importance,

Haman can no longer bear the sight of Mordecai's open defiance. Mordecai stands in contrast to everything the invitation to Esther's private banquet has confirmed to Haman about himself and his position. Haman's joy is quenched by his hot indignation against Mordecai.

What does Haman expect from Mordecai? (v. 9)

What two great spiritual defects become more pronounced in Haman after the banquet? (vv. 9, 11, 12, 13)

What are the two results of Haman's insatiable hatred and pride? (vv. 13, 14)

 PROBING THE DEPTHS

Some scholars assume the height of the proposed gallows to be an exaggeration. The fifty-cubit gallows that Zeresh suggests would be about seventy-five feet high. Although this height seems outlandish and even ridiculous, it is in keeping with Haman's pride and arrogance and quite possible given the Persian flair for doing things in a big way (Esth. 1). It seems Haman wanted to make sure the entire city would see Mordecai's humiliation and tremble at his own power.[4]

Haman reveals his priorities to his wife and friends in a "brag session." Rank Haman's priorities according to the importance he seems to place on each. (vv. 11, 12)

How do these relate to your priorities? If you had to identify the things which are most important to your self-esteem, what would be the top five items on your list?

In what way(s) are Haman's attitudes and actions similar to the rich man's in the parable recorded in Luke 12:16–21?

BIBLE EXTRA

Rebellious and haughty pride is at the root of all sin. Satan fell because of pride (Is. 14:14) as did Adam and Eve (Gen. 3:5). And pride is the first item on the list of the seven things God hates (Prov. 6:16–19).

How does Proverbs 16:5 define pride?

Study the following table:

Characteristics of a Proud Person

Tries to put self in place of God	Gen. 3:5, 6
Sees self as better than others	Luke 18:10–12
Brags about ancestry or heritage	John 8:33
Takes pride in own power and wisdom	Is. 10:12–15
Takes pride in wealth and ability to make money	Ezek. 28:1–7
Takes pride in own spirituality	1 Cor. 4:7

Now look at the effects of pride.

Effects of Pride

Causes quarrels	Prov. 13:10
Deceives the heart	Jer. 49:16
Hardens the heart	Dan. 5:20
Brings shame	Prov. 11:2
Precedes ruin	Prov. 16:18
Brings opposition from God	Prov. 3:34
Brings judgment	Mal. 4:1

FAITH ALIVE

Do any of the characteristics of a proud person describe you? Which one(s)?

Confess your sin in that area, and ask God to cleanse your heart from all unrighteousness. Ask God to help you find your value in relationship to Him instead of the approval of others, material possessions, or power and prestige. Ask Him to give you a heart like Esther's so that you may walk in humility and wisdom controlled by the Holy Spirit.

MORDECAI'S RISE PROCLAIMED (6:1–11)

Proverbs 21:30 states: "There is no wisdom or understanding or counsel against the Lord." This truth is surely proven in the events of chapter 6 and following. The hand of God which was moving in a less visible way in 5:1–8 and 5:9–14, now begins to become evident. Haman's exaggerated sense of self-importance which was stimulated by the private banquet causes him to cast away patience and restraint. After spending the night overseeing the building of the outrageous gallows designed for Mordecai, Haman arrives at the palace before the early crowd of petitioners. But the hand of God had already been working upon King Ahasuerus.

What effect did Esther's banquet seem to have on the king? (6:1)

It was a very serious matter for Ahasuerus to overlook Mordecai's act of five years earlier (2:21–23). Such loyalty was the only assurance the king had against palace intrigues. That Ahasuerus's attendant should pick up this volume of the "Book of Remembrances" was more than a coincidence.

List the other "happenings" which fall in place to fully overturn Haman's murderous plan and bring honor to Mordecai instead.

6:1

6:2, 3

6:4

6:5, 6

6:7–9

6:10, 11

FAITH ALIVE

Malachi 3:16 talks about a "Book of Remembrance" which the Lord keeps containing the words and acts of "those who fear the Lord." Though in the midst of a hostile world where evil sometimes seems to win over good, these people speak often about the Lord to one another and meditate on His name. God calls these people "My jewels" and speaks of rewards which will be given to them (Mal. 3:17, 18; 4:1, 2).

We can be sure, events written in this book will not be forgotten. Will your name appear in that book?

What could God write about you today? How are you showing your love and awe of God?

The author of Esther uses a great deal of irony in this section of text. These "contrasts to the expected outcome" add humor and emphasize human impotence to control the events of the day. Finish the statements which show irony. The first is done for you.

Irony in Esther 6:1–11 Which Suggests the Beginning of Reversal

Esther was chosen by the king for her beauty and sexual appeal. ◄---►	Esther was chosen by God for her courage, wisdom, humility, faith, and ability to lead.
Haman plots Mordecai's death. ◄---►	
Haman went to the palace to speak against Mordecai. ◄---►	
Haman's "mock coronation" was intended to make him appear equal to the king. ◄---►	
Mordecai refused to bow to Haman or show him honor. ◄---►	

HAMAN'S DOOM FORECAST (6:12–14)

The citizenry of Shushan must have viewed Mordecai's ride through town with more than a bit of satisfaction. Surely, the irony of the situation was evident to all. Mordecai, a Jew sentenced to death by Haman's edict, is escorted and served by Haman, the one-who-would-make-himself-great among the people. The differing effect of the ride certainly was dramatic.

The pomp and pageantry so important to Haman seem to have had little effect on Mordecai. Yet, this service so humiliates Haman that he runs to his house "mourning and with his head covered" (v. 12. See 2 Sam. 15:30; Jer. 14:3, 4).

Why does Mordecai quickly return to the gate? What does this show about his values and priorities? (v. 12)

In what ways does Haman's personal crisis present the possibility of both danger and opportunity? (v. 12)

The relationship between Haman and Zeresh appears to be much closer than that of Esther and Ahasuerus. Haman "called for" Zeresh following his success and "hurried to his house" to speak with her in his distress (5:10, 14; 6:12, 13). Yet, Haman's lack of real prestige and honor is even seen in his relationship with his friends and his wife.

Who do his "friends" turn out to be? (v. 13; 5:14)

Since Zeresh seems always to be called with these men, what might her "real" position be in Haman's life?

What are the three progressions in the prediction of Haman's advisors (v. 13)?

How does the answer Zeresh and the wise men give show deceit and disloyalty (5:13, 14; 6:13)?

The "wise men" and "wise woman" who advised Haman had predicted that he would go to the banquet "merrily" (5:14). What adjectives might describe Haman's true state as he is whisked off to the palace with his advisors' words of doom fresh on his ears (v. 14)?

 FAITH ALIVE

What one truth have you learned from Esther 5—6:14 concerning the wisdom of the world and godly wisdom?

The clash between two views of providence is presented throughout the Book of Esther. What have you learned here about God's providence (God's sovereign control)?

What will you do or how will you think differently because of this truth?

How will it affect your life this week?

1. *Spirit-Filled Life Bible* (Nashville: Thomas Nelson Publishers, 1991), 1377, "Word Wealth: Zech. 12:10, grace."

2. Joyce G. Baldwin, *Esther: Introduction and Commentary,* Tyndale Old Testament Commentaries, ed. D. J. Wiseman (Downers Grove: InterVarsity, 1984), 86.

3. Ibid., 87.

4. Ibid., 88.

Lesson 12/Opportunity: Securing Full Petition
(Esther 7:1—8:17)

It is easy to be "fired up" coming out of a prayer meeting or an assembly in which the Spirit has moved in a powerful way. But what lies behind the kind of staying power which causes one to fully give oneself—to stand in the gap until full reversal or physical death comes?

Jesus' example on the eve of His crucifixion offers an answer. John 13:3 reveals three foundational insights which caused Jesus to be fully motivated to do the most menial of human tasks and then bend even lower and offer His sinless life on a criminal's cross. The text states: (1) Jesus knew "that the Father had given all things into His hands," (2) that "He had come from God," and (3) that He "was going to God."

A servant of God has the right heart disposition and motivation when he or she also understands these three things. First, that mission and power to fulfill mission have been given together from God. Second, that his or her life has its origin, foundation, identity, and meaning in God alone. And third, that life with God is his or her one end goal and destination. With this foundation of life and service, distractions, discouragements, temptations, and worldly symbols of power and place become increasingly less influential.

In Esther 7 and 8, Esther exhibits a motivation for the task of intercession which lies beyond herself. Not only does she continue laying down her own life until she secures her full petition for her people, but she begins to demonstrate the characteristics of a servant-leader who is fully yielded to God and mission.

ESTHER'S ACCUSATION (7:1–6)

The writer passes over the events of the second banquet and picks up the story at the course of wines which concludes Esther's second feast (vv. 1, 2). But it is interesting to imagine what was likely going on during the main events of the banquet. Surely Esther, keenly aware of her purpose and mission this day, was alert to every detail of the proceedings. Her queenly robes, her beauty, and gracious manner again remind the king of her relationship to him.

And the king and Haman probably arrived at Esther's apartments with the previous banquet as the context for their expectations. The king, unaware of events outside the palace's inner courts, had likely been delighted by his favorite foods, the wonderful service, and the captivating presence of his queen. Perhaps Ahasuerus remained moderately curious about the queen's request. Surely he was even more favorably inclined toward her this day than previously.

In light of the events immediately preceding Haman's arrival at the banquet, what emotions might he have felt and what thoughts likely occupied his mind during the feast? (6:11–14)

Do you think Haman had given Esther's request much thought? What do you think his level of alertness would be?

As the wine is leisurely enjoyed, Ahasuerus again asks the expected question and again promises Esther a favorable answer to her request. How do his words suggest the way in which he views Esther? (vv. 2; 5:6)

True to her promise, Esther makes her request known. How does her petition show courtesy, respect for Ahasuerus' position, and lack of presumption? (vv. 3, 4; Compare her response to Haman's in 6:7.)

What was Esther's first request and the foundation of her petitions? How does this wording show keen wisdom? (v. 3)

What information is strangely missing from the second request? How does Esther's omission underline her fundamental appeal? (v. 3)

Although Esther uses the language of the decree ("to destroy, to kill, and to annihilate," 3:13; 7:4), she again does not mention the identity of her people or name the decree itself. By this approach, she keeps the issue personal and avoids any hint of accusation against the king (v. 4). She focuses on the king's personal concerns which have been violated. Not only is someone trying to kill the king's queen, but he is also cheating the king!

WORD WEALTH

The Hebrew which stands behind Esther 7:4 is difficult to interpret. **"Could never compensate for the king's loss"** (7:4) is likely the best rendering. It means that even if the king is given a price—even the high price which might be obtained if all Jews were sold into slavery—it would still bring financial loss to Ahasuerus. The continuing revenue from the Jews' taxes would far outweigh any bounty they might bring.[1]

The king may not have assimilated all the import of Esther's words at this point, but his response is personal outrage. How does Ahasuerus describe the act which has been done (v. 5)?

Haman is just beginning to realize Esther is a Jew when Esther's powerful and direct accusation stacks adjectives which describe the heinous nature of his crime. The king's wrath is multiplied, and Haman is "terrified before the king and queen." (v. 6).

WORD WEALTH

"Haman was terrified before the king and queen" (7:6): The Hebrew verb used here means "to be overtaken by sudden terror." Although it is Esther's words and the king's demeanor which Haman might acknowledge as the source of his terror, this word is most often used to describe the reaction of humans—both as sinners and saints—to the awesome and overpowering presence of God.[2] As surely as God has been directing the activities which lead up to this moment, He has also empowered Esther's words which bring the sentence of death to this enemy of God and His people.

HAMAN'S END (7:7—8:2)

It seems unusual for the king to delay his action and rush to the palace garden (v. 7; 1:12–22; 3:8–11). Yet, there was much to think about. How Ahasuerus put together Haman's attempt to kill the queen and the Jews, the assassination plot of Teresh and Bigthana, and Mordecai's reporting of the conspiracy is unknown. If the king had any uncertainty about his action, it was solved when he returned from the garden! Haman's terror causes him to act very foolishly (vv. 7, 8).

BEHIND THE SCENES

Haman's invitation to Esther's banquet was a high honor and an unusual privilege (5:2). Harem regulations were very rigid. Even as queen, Esther was not allotted the freedom of the palace but was restricted to the women's quarters and courtyard. Only the king's trusted eunuchs were allowed to enter the queen's house or the harem or have any contact with the king's queen or concubines. To approach the couch upon which Esther reclined was a breach of palace etiquette, but to fall upon her couch or to touch her was an affront to the king himself—perhaps even an act of treason.

If Ahasuerus needed a scapegoat to exonerate himself from his part in the edict against the Jews, he had one now. Haman's death sentence was solidly sealed by this improper act! The covering of Haman's face is a sign that he was condemned to death.[3]

How does Haman's own boasting among the king's servants provide the tool for the ultimate irony? (vv. 9, 10; see 1:10)

FAITH ALIVE

Two key truths are presented in Esther 7:10. Read the following references and write these truths in your own words.

Truth 1: (Ps. 94:23; Prov. 16:4)

Truth 2: (Ps. 7:16; Prov. 11:5, 6)

How are these truths important to you personally?

To what actions do they call you? How are you incorporating or how will you incorporate this action into your daily life?

According to Persian law, the state possessed the right to confiscate all property belonging to a criminal.[4] Although Ahasuerus had earlier been tempted by Haman's great wealth, the king gives Haman's full estate to Esther on the very day of Haman's hanging. Perhaps the king felt guilty about receiving Haman's goods for himself since he too had been involved in passing legislation to kill his own queen.

In what other way did the king honor Esther? (8:1)

How did Esther honor Mordecai? What characteristic of a servant-leader is illustrated by her actions? (8:1, 2)

In what way do the events of Esther 8:1, 2 test the motive and mission of Esther and Mordecai?

 PROBING THE DEPTHS

There are many points at which the motive and mission of an intercessor is tested. At each of these points, the intercessor is asked to move deeper into the purposes of God. And at each of these points the would-be intercessor is challenged with a new "price" for that commitment. First, the intercessor is asked to open the heart to a desperate need and answer the call to intercede. Second, the intercessor is asked to fully identify with the pain and peril of those for whom she intercedes. Third, the minister must sensitively follow the Spirit's lead to completion of the task of deliverance and reversal.

All along the way, these commitments must be made again and again at new levels. The heart can become hardened. The intercessor can pull away from the pain or humiliation of others. One can become more self-centered than mission-centered. A life that could be greatly used by God to deliver a nation or a people can become sidetracked by bitterness, discouragement, or the desire for approval, power, prestige, or wealth. Even the "perks" of the first stages of reversal (such as the personal reversal Esther and Mordecai experienced) may cause one to forget about others at the grassroots level who have not yet experienced full reversal.

 FAITH ALIVE

Have you heard the call to intercede for a nation or people or heal an area of brokenness in the body of Christ? At what stage of intercession are you? What are your particular challenges to that call now?

Ask God for the power and anointing of His Spirit to help you to finish your course like Esther and Mordecai.

One of the truths which may be gleaned from Esther 8:1, 2 is recorded in Proverbs 13:22. Write that verse below.

ESTHER'S PETITION (8:3–8)

The first verses of the eighth chapter of Esther describe the extraordinary personal favor Esther found in the king's sight (8:1, 2). The following section (8:3–8) proves that Esther finds her foundation for mission outside personal gain. Her zeal for God's plan of deliverance is not diminished by the power and wealth she is given. Esther takes advantage of her window of favor in order to secure her full petition for her people.

How does Esther's second presentation of her petition differ from that of her earlier requests? Why do you suppose this is so? (8:3–6; 7:3, 4)

How does Esther refer to Haman? What wisdom is again shown by this approach to her public appeal? (8:3, 5; see also Prov. 31:11, 12, 26)

What two meanings could lie behind the king's words recorded in 8:7? Based on verse 8, which is the more appropriate?

The Hebrew word order of Esther 8:8 makes the plural "you" emphatic, showing that King Ahasuerus empowers Esther and Mordecai together (see also 9:32).[5] In what way(s) is this action appropriate given the behind-the-scene activity?

The king's reminder that "whatever is written in the king's name and sealed with the king's signet ring no one can revoke" tells Esther and Mordecai that the right given to the Jews' enemies cannot itself be taken away. However, another decree may cancel out its effectiveness. And a new decree favoring the Jews would indicate the king's disposition toward them and encourage others to follow suit.

THE GREAT REVERSAL (8:9–17)

In this section of text, the writer emphasizes the great reversal of the Jews' situation by using a special writing technique. The author pens verses 9–17 as a paraphrase of the chapter 3 account of Haman's decree. In some places the wording is almost identical, showing a point by point avenging of the edict written against the Jews. A preference for the Jews and the superiority of the importance of this new decree is seen in its two additions. First, the Jews will both hear the proclamation and read the new decree in Hebrew (8:9; 3:12). Second, the decree will not only be hastened to the ends of the Persian Empire, but the king's royal racehorses will deliver it (8:10, 14; 3:15).

When did the writing and dispatch of this counter-decree take place? (v. 9)

 BIBLE EXTRA

"The month of Sivan, on the twenty-third day" (8:9): Haman sealed and dispatched his decree on the thirteenth day of the first month, Nisan (3:7, 12). Mordecai's decree was written on the twenty-third day of Sivan, the third month of the Babylonian calendar. Thus, approximately seventy days elapsed between Haman's and Mordecai's decrees. Some commentators see this period of time as symbolic of the seventy years of the Babylonian captivity.[6] What message of warning and hope might underlie this symbolism?

What two actions are the Jews given legal permission to perform? Are these offensive or defensive strategies (8:11)?

The wording of 8:11 appears to be a rewording of Haman's decree. The Jews were not given the right to "destroy, kill, and annihilate" children and women, but rather they could protect their women, children, and possessions (see 9:6, 15).

What was the decree's stated purpose (v. 13)?

 AT A GLANCE

The response to the decree could immediately be gauged by the reaction in Shushan. Compare the responses to Haman's and Mordecai's edicts in Shushan and among the Jews in the provinces by completing the chart below.

Haman's Edict		Mordecai's Edict	
The city of Shushan: "was perplexed"	3:15	The city of Shushan:	8:15
Among the Jews was: mourning fasting weeping and wailing sackcloth	4:3	The Jews had:	8:16, 17
--------------------------		"In addition, many of the people of the land became Jews, because the fear of the Jews fell upon them." Esther 8:17	

Write Proverbs 11:10, which aptly summarizes the information in the chart.

Mordecai left the citadel that evening in royal robes and a prime minister's crown (v. 15). After completing her mission and facilitating Mordecai's appointment, Esther seems to have disappeared momentarily into the background. Esther's willingness to use her influence, material assets, and intellect to bring about the good of God's people while maintaining a humble and sensitive heart marks her as a true servant-leader.

1. *Spirit-Filled Life Bible* (Nashville: Thomas Nelson Publishers, 1991), 703, note on Esther 7:4.

2. R. Laird Harris, Gleason L. Archer, Jr., and Bruce K. Waltke, eds., *Theological Word-book of the Old Testament* (Chicago: Moody Press, 1980), 122, no. 265.

3. *Spirit-Filled Life Bible*, 703, note on Esther 7:8.

4. F. B. Huey, Jr., *Esther*, vol. 4, The Expositor's Bible Commentary, ed. Frank E. Gaebelein (Grand Rapids: Zondervan, 1988), 828.

5. Joyce G. Baldwin, *Esther: An Introduction and Commentary*, Tyndale Old Testament Commentaries, ed. D. J. Wiseman (Downers Grove: InterVarsity, 1984), 96.

6. *Spirit-Filled Life Bible*, 704, note on Esther 8:9.

Lesson 13/Opportunity: Maintaining Victory
(Esther 9:1—10:3)

It is rare to turn on the radio or pick up a newspaper today without finding an account of someone who has fallen from a high position. Yesterday's political favorite finds his career over in one day as reports of unethical alliances, embezzlement, or immoral behavior hit the headlines. Others quickly fall out of favor with their politically powerful colleagues or a special interest group and begin a downhill slide. Those who continue in office unscathed seem a definite minority. And the same political intrigues and ethical dilemmas common to the secular world are found on a lesser scale among leaders in denominations and churches.

Yet the story of Mordecai and Esther shows that godly leaders can not only maintain their level of authority and influence, but grow in favor and power. Through the disciplines of integrity, unity, and selfless service, Esther and Mordecai benefit the kingdom of Persia and help the Jews remember and maintain the victory God gives to them. Their influence and message of hope continues on today through the remembrance and celebration of their story.

MAINTAINING VICTORY THROUGH INTEGRITY (9:1–16)

The multiple reversals which began with Esther's acceptance of her ministry call and the prayer and fasting of the people (4:14–17) find their fulfillment in this section of the text. The day which Haman—by the casting of the lot—had determined to be the most favorable for the extinction of the Jews, becomes the day "the opposite occurred" and "the Jews themselves overpowered those who hated them" (v. 1).

Write the four phrases which describe how God controlled the day and gave favor to the Jews and to Mordecai on behalf of the Jews (vv. 2, 3).

1.

2.

3.

4.

What inference could be made concerning Esther's royal position and authority during the nine-month interim between the publishing of the second decree and the day of its execution (vv. 12–14)?

Mordecai's experience during the same time period seems to parallel or even exceed Esther's. What explanation can be given for his swift advancement (vv. 3, 4)?

BIBLE EXTRA

Optional: Study the "fear of God's people."
Found in Esther (7:6; 9:2, 3)
Prophesied by Moses (Ex. 15:14–17)
Promised by God (Ex. 30:21ff; 23:27)
Proclaimed before battle (Deut. 2:25)
Experienced during early days of Church (Acts 5:1–11)

Then think about these questions:
(1) How might the "fear of them" (v. 2) be more clearly defined or described? In other words, what or who is this "fear"?

(2) What does the "fear" do or cause among God's enemies?

(3) What kind of relationship to God must a corporate people have in order to experience this type of manifestation of God's presence?

(4) How is personal and corporate "fear of God" related to the manifestation of the "fear of God's people" among their enemies?

Verse 5 is both a concise summary of the Jews' general activity throughout the provinces (vv. 1–4) and an introduction to the more specific accounts which follow concerning Shushan (vv. 6–15) and the provinces (v. 16). The phrase "with the stroke of the sword with slaughter and destruction" reports a threefold overthrow of "destroy, kill, and annihilate" in Haman's decree.

WORD WEALTH

The phrase **"did what they pleased"** (9:5) may sound ruthless and vicious to our ears. However, it must be defined by what follows in 9:6–16 and the general context of the Book of Esther. The phrase bears the broad sense of a fulfillment of

Mordecai's words that "relief and deliverance" (4:14) would come to the Jews. Now, it is clear that this "wide space" or "relief" comes through the Jews' legal right and freedom to fully defend themselves. The Jews' victory was over "those who sought their harm" (v. 2), "those who hated them" (v. 5), "men" (v. 6), "the ten sons of Haman, . . . the enemy of the Jews" (vv. 7–10). Nowhere is ruthless slaughter of children and women suggested as Haman had decreed against the Jews, but rather victory over able warriors.

 ### BEHIND THE SCENES

The English text of verses 6–10 cannot communicate the vivid message presented in the Hebrew text. After the numerical account of the slaughter in Shushan (v. 6), the names of Haman's ten sons are listed in the shape of an impalement pole or a gallows (vv. 7–9). This dramatic visual image is followed in verse 10 by a genealogy: "the ten sons of Haman the son of Hammedatha, the enemy of the Jews—they killed." Without its addition, one can almost hear the title "the Agagite" in the genealogy and trace Haman's line all the way back to King Agag—proverbial enemy of the Jews who brought Saul's downfall when Saul coveted the Agagites' goods and rebelliously failed to utterly destroy their king.

What message do you suppose this unusual inscription was intended to impart to the Jews who read it? (vv. 6–10)

What message does it contain for Christians? For you personally?

PROBING THE DEPTHS

Esther's request for a second day of slaughter (vv. 11–15) has raised the eyebrows of some interpreters. They have shouted labels like: "Bloodthirsty!" or "Inhumane!" or "Pagan!" But noticing the request's placement right after the "gallows" and genealogy causes it to make more sense. Do Esther's requests serve to underline the message of the visual image and genealogy and reinforce the fact that God's enemies are to be pursued and destroyed to the very last one? Does Esther's action suggest something important about spiritual warfare and intercession? Does it suggest the "Great Intercessor" who was to come who would destroy the enemy to the last one?

In contrast to Haman or pagan Ahasuerus, Esther is the symbol of wisdom, sensitive servant-leadership, and unity among God's people. For her request to be frivolously uttered or vicious would be out of keeping with her role in the account. The reader is not told everything, but surely Haman's home, the home of his ten sons, and the citadel of the Empire would be the stronghold of opposition to the Jews! Perhaps a known conspiracy is brewing among the enemy, who is poised to make one last-ditch effort.

Whatever the interpretation one finds here, Esther's request does not compare in cruelty to the greedy plunder of the Jews and the heinous annihilation of hundreds of thousands of women and children which Haman proposed and others attempted.

How did the Jews maintain their purpose and show their integrity (vv. 10, 15, 16; 8:11)?

How did this restraint prove a good witness?

If the Jews had **not** exceeded the morality of the law in this way, how might their action affect them politically? In their business and personal relationships in the community?

How did this refusal to touch the plunder—or property of their enemies—show obedience to Scripture and sensitivity to conscience? (1 Sam. 15:1–3, 17–23)

 FAITH ALIVE

Look up the definition of "integrity" in a good dictionary. List its various applications. Using these aspects of the word, write your own definition of "Christian integrity."

In order to maintain an unsullied victory during the process and aftermath of reversal, the Jews demonstrated righteous action which was obedient to Scripture and sensitive to conscience and their witness in a secular world.
How might a local church or denomination apply these guidelines when working to reverse racial or gender prejudice within its ministry and mission?

Look at an area in your life in which you have desired victory. Have your actions shown obedience to Scripture (foundation) and sensitivity to conscience (motive) and witness (effects on others)?

What needs to change? Commit yourself to that in prayer.

AT A GLANCE

Major concepts learned throughout the Book of Esther are presented again in 9:1–16. Read the verses again, and write these concepts in the chart.

Subject	Verse	Concept or Lesson Learned
God's Sovereignty	1	
The Origin of Favor	2, 3	
God's Choice of Leaders and the Purpose of Favor	4, 12–14 (also see 9:25; 10:3)	

MAINTAINING VICTORY THROUGH REMEMBRANCE AND CELEBRATION (9:17–28)

This section of the ninth chapter of Esther describes the establishment of the Feast of Purim. The explanation of when, why, and how the tradition of Purim came about and the exhortation to continue its celebration indicate the original purpose for the writing of the Book of Esther.

Verses 17–19 describe the facts included in a letter Mordecai sent to the Jews throughout the Persian Empire in order to establish uniform celebration of the Feast of Purim.

What was the character of the two-day memorial to be? (v. 22) To what United States or international holiday might it be compared? Why?

What is to be remembered and what is to be celebrated? (vv. 24, 25)

True to the Book of Esther's distinctiveness, the name of God is not mentioned in the motivation for the installation of this religious holiday (vv. 24, 25). However, the phrases "plotted against . . . and had cast Pur" (v. 24) beg the reader to supply the counterphrases "God controlled events . . . and the people fasted." Haman's faith in the "lot" is countered by Jewish faith in the sovereignty of the "hidden" God. This God, no longer identified by the temple in Jerusalem, hides among His people and defends them in this foreign land. This God, when sought, may be found. Perhaps the very "unspokenness" of God's name is, in a sense, plainly "spoken" in the Feast's name.

WORD WEALTH

Haman cast **Pur**, that is, "the lot." But the Jewish holiday celebrated on the 14th and 15th of Adar (one month before Passover) is called **Purim**, or "lots." The Feast of Purim (POOR im) is not named for Haman's lot, but an additional "lot." In a sense, God was the "unknown factor" which Haman did not take into account![1]

Who are the "others" who might participate in Purim with the Jews? (v. 27, 8:17)

What is to be the extent of the commemoration of Purim? (vv. 27, 28)

WORD WEALTH

Every generation and family (9:28): "Generation" (*dor*) means an age, a revolution of time, or a life span. It comes from a verb meaning to dwell or to circle and indicates "a coming full circle in life" either the time from birth to death or the time from one's conception in the womb until the time one produces offspring. "Family" (*mishpachah*) indicates a type, class, or kind of people related in some way and may mean a tribe, clan, immediate family, or whole nation. Thus, Esther 9:27, 28 urges all Jews of all time from every family to the last generation throughout the whole Earth to remember and celebrate the Feast of Purim.[2]

The Feast of Purim has not been forgotten by Jews of this modern age. Every year at Purim, Jewish leaders around the world read the Book of Esther to the enthusiastic crowds which fill the synagogues. People cheer for Mordecai as his deeds are mentioned. But each of the fifty-three times Haman—the arch-enemy of the Jews—is named, the same crowds boo and jeer, blow horns and shake rattles to drown out his name.[3]

In light of the events of World War II and the seemingly endless conflicts surrounding the modern nation of Israel, one can see why remembering the events recorded in the Book of Esther is important to Jews. Purim forever holds out the hope that their enemies' plans will be overturned, that God controls the lot, and that the Jews will never be exterminated from the earth.

 FAITH ALIVE

But why is remembrance of the events of Esther important to Christians? What difference does it make today that these events took place?

How is your life or faith enhanced by knowing this account? Why is it cause for celebration?

How does remembrance and celebration of the Great Reversal worked by Jesus Christ take place? How important is this commemoration to our faith?

Scripture shows the danger of forgetting the salvific acts of God and becoming dissected from the story of salvation history. We, like Israel of old and the early church, have a "story" made up of the account of God's mighty acts among

us, the corporate body of Christ, the local church and denomination. How are the mighty reversals from God which are
peculiar to your local church remembered and celebrated?

What accounts of mighty reversals worked by God in
your life or that of your ancestors are important to hand on to
your children as part of your family heritage and tradition?

How will you remember and celebrate this family heritage so that the story is not lost?

MAINTAINING YOUR VICTORY THROUGH UNITY (9:29–32)

This last section of chapter 9 functions to further
strengthen the case for observance of the Feast of Purim and to
prove its authenticity as a Jewish tradition. Here, Esther and
Mordecai are again seen acting with a unity and mutual support characteristic of godly leaders.

Who wrote the first letter concerning Purim? (9:20) Who
is the author of this second letter about Purim? (vv. 29, 32)

What is the purpose of Queen Esther's letter? (v. 31, 32)

How do Esther and Mordecai demonstrate their mutual
support in this section of the text? (vv. 30, 31) How is this
same kind of mutuality seen in chapters 2, 4, and 8 and implied
in 9:11–14?

Notice the order in which Esther and Mordecai's names are listed in verses 29 and 31. What significance does this order seem to have?

In Esther 8:8, King Ahasuerus is shown to give Esther and Mordecai like authority to pen the decree which brought reversal. But Esther 8:9 describes only Mordecai's part in the document's creation. Given your conclusion to the previous question and this fact, how might you relate these ideas to Paul's exhortation concerning leadership and unity recorded in 1 Corinthians 3:5–8?

WORD WEALTH

Written in the book (9:32): Two questions arise from this phrase. What is the authority of Esther's writing, and in what book was it written? The Hebrew verb is not helpful here since it is a general word for "write, record, enroll."[4] Fortunately, other clues concerning the authority of Esther's writing are given elsewhere. The Hebrew verb of 9:29 is feminine singular indicating that although Mordecai is "with" Esther, she is the one who wrote with "full authority"—or "the power and authority of a kingdom or a ruler" (v. 29, see Dan 11:17).[5] "The book" denotes a particular and well-known book in which an authoritative "decree" or "command" (v. 32) would logically be written. Most likely, it is the legal record of the Medes and Persians since Mordecai uses his official position to send Esther's decree throughout the provinces (v. 30). Other less likely possibilities: a Jewish chronicle of some sort or the scroll of Esther itself.

PROBING THE DEPTHS

Although Persia was a paternalistic society and King Ahasuerus himself used women as objects for his sexual enjoyment, he did not seem to think it strange to promote Esther to new levels of leadership when her wisdom and giftedness became apparent. And Mordecai yielded to Esther's obvious anointing to act as intercessor. With an amazing and beautiful unity, the two Jews worked together for the good of their people. Esther gave preference to Mordecai, and at times he preferred her.

Given the examples of Esther's inspired wisdom, the religious and political leadership of women like Deborah and Huldah, and modern leaders like Maria B. Woodworth-Etter and Marilyn Hickey, why is it so difficult for the body of Christ to receive the leadership of women? Could a local church's refusal of women's speaking and leadership gifts be defined as "quenching the Spirit" (1 Thess. 5:19–22)? How is the body of Christ affected when God-given gifts of leadership are not allowed to operate? Do unity issues like racism and exclusion of women from the full ministry and mission of the church severely inhibit corporate outpourings of the Spirit?

MAINTAINING VICTORY THROUGH SELFLESS SERVICE (10:1–3)

This last chapter of Esther describes the greatness of Mordecai and the heritage he left to the generations who followed him. It does that first by relating the greatness of Ahasuerus. Certainly the king of Persia benefitted from the wise leadership of Mordecai (see Gen. 41). Ahasuerus's imposition of forced labor throughout his kingdom emphasizes his power and the extent of his domain (v. 1; 10:1)[6] Mention of the chronicles adds the historical authority of written record to the greatness which is described.

Why would God be inclined to give great favor and high position to a person like Mordecai?

List the five accolades given Mordecai in verse 3.

1.

2.

3.

4.

5.

Like Nehemiah after him, Mordecai grasped opportunity in order to "seek the good of his people" (v. 3; Neh. 2:10). In seeking their good, he was able to speak "peace to all his countrymen." Generations of Jews had a different and better future because of his leadership and intentional protection and care. And perhaps he and Esther helped preserve the very ancestors of the Messiah.

 WORD WEALTH

"Speaking peace" (10:3): "Peace," *shalom,* is defined as completeness, wholeness, peace, health, welfare, safety, soundness, tranquillity, prosperity, perfectness, fullness, rest, harmony, the absence of agitation or discord. It comes from a verb meaning "to be complete, perfect, full." Thus, *shalom* is the absence of war and conflict which the entire human race seeks. Jesus is the ultimate "shalom"—the great peace-bringer. At His birth, the angels rejoiced saying, "Glory to God in the highest; and on earth peace, goodwill toward men!" (Luke 2:14–17; compare Is. 9:7).[7]

FAITH ALIVE

Like Mordecai, you too have opportunity to seek the good of others. How are you seeking the welfare of your employer? Fellow employees? Community? Church? Family?

Though Mordecai worked for the good of the people of Persia and the king, his greatest sense of responsibility was to his own people. His motivation to seek their good affected generations of Jews. How do your priorities line up with this order of things? Are family and church at the top of your list?

Do you "speak peace" to those around you? How are you letting Christ live in you to bring wholeness to your spouse? Children? Church?

Are you a balm which takes away discord? A "safe harbor" for broken and hurting people? One who enhances others with intentional and sincere edification? Confess areas where you fail to create unity and wholeness. Ask God to speak His peace into your life in a new way that you will truly be a peace-bringer in these relationships and situations. God will begin to work in these areas. Be sensitive to the Holy Spirit and yield yourself to God's work.

Pick one family member and one church relationship to whom you will intentionally "speak peace" for the next two weeks. Ask God to give you insight into needs, areas that require preventative care, ways in which you can encourage, build up, and bless those persons. Record your insights and experiences in a journal so you can see the hand of God more clearly and testify of the "shalom" God brings to you and flows through you.

FAITH ALIVE

Review of the Book of Esther: Throughout the Book of Esther, we have seen ways in which we can use opportunity to work with God to bring great reversals in individual lives and in a corporate people. Sometimes opportunity is plain and clear (Esth. 4), at other times it is more difficult to recognize opportunities as they present themselves (Esth. 2). The Book of Esther shows that when we yield ourselves to God in every situation—even during the times when God seems hidden from view, it opens the wonderful possibility of being used in ways which affect generations to come. And we ourselves are gloriously transformed during that process!

Flip back through the lessons on Esther. Review the opportunities which may challenge you at different points in the ministry of intercession. In your study notebook or a journal of your spiritual journey, write the titles of lessons 7—13. Next to each one record one major personal learning.

Close your review with a prayer. (You may also wish to write the prayer as a record of your thanksgiving and commitment to God.) Thank God for the reversals He has already worked in your life and those He is now preparing. Express your desire to be used as His instrument of reversal and deliverance. Thank Him for the opportunities He is even now setting in your path. Ask Him to make you alert to each one.

1. "Purim," *Nelson's Illustrated Bible Dictionary* (Nashville: Thomas Nelson Publishers, 1986).

2. *Spirit-Filled Life Bible* (Nashville: Thomas Nelson Publishers, 1991), 705, "Word Wealth: Esth. 9:28, generation." Ibid., 22, "Word Wealth: Gen. 12:3, families."

3. Mark Roberts, *Ezra, Nehemiah, Esther,* Mastering the Old Testament, ed. Lloyd J. Ogilvie (Dallas: Word Publishing, 1993), 363, 433.

4. R. Laird Harris, Gleason L. Archer, Jr., and Bruce K. Waltke, eds., *Theological Wordbook of the Old Testament* (Chicago: Moody Press, 1980), 458–459, no. 1053.

5. Ibid., 979–980, no. 2542a. Joyce G. Baldwin, *Esther: An Introduction and Commentary,* Tyndale Old Testament of Commentaries, ed. D. J. Wiseman (Downers Grove: InterVarsity Press, 1984), 110.

6. *Spirit-Filled Life Bible,* 706, note on Esther 10:1.

7. Ibid., 1334, "Word Wealth: Nah. 1:15, peace."